Nigel Foster's

SEA KAYAKING

Second Edition

Nigel Foster

West Sussex, England

Old Saybrook, Connecticut

Published by:

Fernhurst Books
Duke's Path, High Street, Arundel, West Sussex, BN18 9AJ, England

The Globe Pequot Press
6 Business Park Road, P.O. Box 833, Old Saybrook, Connecticut 06475-0833

Cover design by Adam Schwartzman. Front cover photos by Terry Harlowe. Back cover photos by Chris
Cunningham. Text photos by Julia Claxton, Neil Ryder, and Nigel Foster, with additional photos by Drew
Delaney and Mark Harrison.

Text edited and designed by Joyce Chester.

The author would like to thank Chris Hawkesworth of Wild Water for his assistance with equipment, and all
those who gave their time to help with the photographic sessions.

Fernhurst Books would like to thank Geoff Good of the British Canoe Union for his helpful comments on the
manuscript.

Library of Congress Cataloging-in-Publication Data
Foster, Nigel.
    [Sea kayaking]
    Nigel Foster's sea kayaking / by Nigel Foster. 2nd ed.
    p. cm.
    ISBN 0-7627-0132-3
    1. Sea kayaking. I. Title.
  GV788 . 5 . F77 1997
  797 . 1'224 – dc21
                              97-13211
                                 CIP

British Library Cataloguing-in-Publication Data
A catalogue record for this book is available from the British Library

ISBN 1-898660-42-5

Printed in Hong Kong

Second Edition/First printing

Contents _____

Sea kayaking offers a magical kind of freedom. You see the shore from a different perspective. You are master of your own craft, and you move at your own pace across the water. You also, however, can face danger at any moment, and knowing what to do when that occurs can make the difference between life and death.

When I began kayaking as a teenager, I learned by trial and error. I used to wheel my canvas-and-wood kayak two miles down the road in southern England and head off along the coast. The air was full of the sound of the shore-break throwing and dragging at the flint pebbles, the smell of seaweed in the sun, the dazzling glare from the white chalk cliffs. My imagination was fired! I loved the feel of the kayak on the water, the freedom of controlling a craft that responded to my every movement, the tang of anxiety I felt being offshore with only my skill to keep me from harm. I was young and enthusiastic, but also, as I realize now, lucky. I used my paddle inefficiently, and I made mistakes that put me in danger that I never anticipated.

This book covers much of the groundwork that I learned the hard way. It can teach you what to expect from the sea. It will explain paddling techniques that will allow you to move in harmony with the sea. Hopefully, it will help you bypass my mistakes and narrow shaves.

Whether you prefer gliding in a serene seascape, cruising on a mirror surface, or navigating the rough turbulence of the exposed rocky shoreline, the surf line, or a tidal rapid, you will need to know how to anticipate sea conditions. You will need an understanding of how tidal streams, weather, swells, and different types of shoreline create certain situations. This book is intended to help you, the paddler, in these efforts.

To get the most from my work, you will need to practice the techniques I have described and take time to understand the theory I explain. I have packed this book from cover to cover with detail that I find invaluable. You probably will need to reread some sections, maybe many times over, with your paddle in hand, before you are confident. However, the time and effort you put in will be rewarded when you are on the water.

A big difference between a beginner and an experienced paddler is awareness: the ability to observe all that is around, interpret what is happening, and respond accordingly. This book will be your guide on how to be at one with your craft, be at one with the sea, and be at one with nature.

Although I have been actively involved in sea kayaking for nearly thirty years, I am still learning more and discovering new experiences. I have spent years instructing and guiding groups in places like Iceland, Arctic Norway, and Scotland. I have taught in Holland, Denmark, Finland, and Canada and have lectured at sea-kayak symposia from Ireland to Sweden, Florida to Washington. My love of the sport is greater now than ever.

I wish you safe and happy paddling.

Introduction

It was a warm spring day in North Wales. Four of us had launched our kayaks from the corner of a steep shingle beach and crossed the calm water to the edge of the narrow sound to survey the choppy water of the tidal race that ran between the mainland and the small island, just half a mile away. From our previous calculations, we knew that the tide would now be running at almost its maximum rate, so we aimed our kayaks well out into the sea towards the north of the island, watching with satisfaction as our view of the island quickly changed as we drifted sideways in the tide. As we neared the island shore, a slight change in course enabled us to keep a rock on the foreshore in line with the cliff behind, stopping our sideways drift in the tide and bringing us neatly to the shore. Behind us a small yacht was making use of the four knot tide to help its engine as it chugged along the coast in search of a breeze.

Twenty minutes later, we relaxed in our kayaks off the farthest end of the island, just below the steep limestone cliffs of the promontory, and watched the whirring flight of puffins and guillemots criss-crossing overhead, and the stiff-winged gliding fulmars carving graceful turns across the water. It was an idyllic morning.

Then as we waited a whiskered face emerged from the water, gazing at the sleek shapes of our craft. Then more heads appeared around us, bright attentive eyes switching their attention from kayak to kayak. I recognized the nearest one as the female I had been watching here for weeks. I talked quietly; a lot of nonsense to my smiling companions, but apparently reassuring to the seal who swam confidently towards me and slipped silently beneath my kayak. Ten minutes passed as we manoeuvred our kayaks gently around the rocks with our attentive companions. Then, with a boldness I had not seen before, the most confident seal approached my bow, rolled gently onto her back and inched slowly along the length of my hull, pulling herself along by her flippers. When she next appeared it was by my paddle blade which was resting on the water. She investigated with her nose, her big brown eyes watching me cautiously. A seal nearby dived with a loud splash and she was gone, speeding through the water. Moments later she was returning again to her investigations. I was spellbound.

Several years and 2000 miles away in Newfoundland, Tim and I sped through the fog with a freshening breeze at our backs. We had been there for several weeks, cruising the coast with our camping equipment loaded into the watertight compartments in our kayaks. The weather forecast warned of gales, which would clear the fog, but for the moment we kept a steady compass bearing that would bring us to Bell Island in another hour. Before we reached the island, the fog had cleared, but the wind had kicked up a steep sea. A couple of well-timed paddle strokes and our kayaks would surge forward on the face of a wave, whereupon light paddle control with a stern rudder would keep us on our course. A few hours later the wind was howling at gale force off the end of Cape Saint Francis. Yet here, our intended landing place, huge Atlantic breakers creamed over the rocks, sending great plumes of spray drifting offshore in the wind. We had been

prepared for the wind but the swell was unexpected. Yet we needed to land. Down the rocky shore ran a narrow slipway made of trimmed logs. The rocks of the beach were clearly too large to permit a safe landing in this sea. The slipway would be our only possibility. We sat beyond the break line and watched the waves. First a large set of huge rollers thundered in to the shore, then a short lull of smaller waves before the next set of rollers. We waited for the next lull, then I sprinted towards the shore, reversing smartly to avoid being carried in by each breaker. Approaching the slipway I stalled once more to allow a wave to break beneath my bow, and paddled forward to be swept in on the back of the wave. Draw-stroking quickly to avoid being carried sideways over the edge of the slipway, I waited until the wave began to drain away before slipping from my cockpit and hauling my kayak out of harm's reach. I was ashore.

Tim came next. With perfect control he chose another lull and sped towards me as I waited on the slip. Using his well-practised technique, he was soon safely beside me. In high spirits we strolled off to look for somewhere suitable to pitch our tent.

Sea kayaking safely requires a combination of understanding, planning and technical skill. You need to understand tides, weather and route planning, and you need to know what causes waves and how they will affect you. Your equipment needs to be well thought out and appropriate, and your paddling skill should take account of changing conditions.

Sea kayaking can be a truly magical experience if you approach it correctly. It can bring you intimately close to wildlife and the elements, and to yourself. However, it is prudent to ask yourself 'What if . . . ' This book sets out to answer that and many of the other questions you may have. Throughout this book I assume that you, the reader, have a basic level of kayaking skill, as detailed in my book *Canoeing: A Beginner's Guide to the Kayak*.

1 Sea kayaks and fittings

There is a wide diversity of craft that can all be called sea kayaks. Each design necessarily compromises between different characteristics, so as sea paddlers you need to decide which characteristics are most desirable for your own purposes and ability level. No one kayak will be ideal for everybody! To choose a suitable sea kayak, you need to be clear about what sort of sea kayaking you might want to do in the future as well as what your immediate needs are. In this chapter I will look at general design characteristics, and also ways in which sea kayaks may be fitted out for the sea.

Hull shape

The shape of the hull determines the performance of a kayak. Broad, flattish hulls tend to be initially stable (initial stability is the 'bolt upright' stability, whereas secondary stability is the stability of the craft when it is leaned over) and manoeuvrable, and kindly to beginners. A degree of *rocker* curvature of the hull upwards towards the bow and stern from the centre) will also increase the manoeuvrability of the kayak while it is upright. However, such kayaks lack directional stability, becoming difficult to keep on course in choppy or windy conditions, and the greater the degree of rocker, the slower the kayak will be.

Narrow and more rounded hulls with little or no rocker tend to be more directionally stable, faster and need less effort to paddle. However, they have less initial stability, are less manoeuvrable when upright, and are less forgiving to beginners. They normally turn easily when leaned, whereupon good secondary stability is

Above *A range of different sea kayak designs.*

Broader, flatter hulls (left) have more initial stability than narrow, more rounded hulls.

Bow shapes. More buoyant bows give a drier ride, but have greater windage.

an asset. Unfortunately, not many kayaks of this kind have a high degree of secondary stability! One way of increasing secondary stability is to incorporate a chine into the hull design. Chines are angles in the hull, such as those created in seal-skin kayaks where the skin crosses a longitudinal wooden stringer. When the chine is tilted into the water, a point of extra stability is reached, and when the flatter hull side above the chine is resting on the water, a further point of stability is found.

For the beginner, would the best choice be a kayak that is easy to handle initially, but becomes harder work when the conditions get rougher, or one that is more difficult to master but handles better when conditions get rougher? One way in which a kayak that is adversely affected by wind and waves can be made to handle more easily is to add a retractable skeg, or a rudder. Both these accessories are helpful to kayaks that show a tendency to turn upwind. Neither works well with kayaks that turn downwind. Fortunately most stable kayak designs tend to turn upwind. Quite a lot of beginners choose stable kayaks initially, and replace them with more directionally stable ones later.

Expedition kayaks can carry camping equipment and provisions for an extended period, and still perform well. Such kayaks are often designed with deeper hulls and are best suited to loaded travel as they can present a high profile to the wind when empty. Conversely, low capacity kayaks usually handle best when empty or lightly laden, and may wallow when heavily laden.

The volume of the bow of a sea kayak influences its behaviour in waves. A low volume bow will tend to plough into waves and plunge deeply in troughs, whereas a higher volume bow will rise to give a drier ride over waves, and will plunge less. Excessively high bows can cause windage problems.

Double sea kayaks

A double sea kayak is generally more stable than a single-seater. Because it is more difficult to allow for the different weights of paddlers in the front and rear, a rudder is usually necessary when it's windy. A double requires cooperation between two paddlers and, naturally, needs two people. For these reasons it is often purchased in addition to single-seaters rather than as an alternative.

Below *Double sea kayak.*

When fitted out well, a double is eminently seaworthy. With the extra paddler you can maintain a good speed. A double enables a less experienced or injured paddler to keep pace with a more experienced or a fitter paddler.

There are several characteristics of doubles that need to be considered.

1 Windage is greater than for singles. When you are broadside to the wind, you must maintain a greater angle into the wind to follow a similar course. This is particularly noticeable when singles are being paddled alongside doubles.

2 Whereas a single kayak has the greatest weight in one position in the centre, allowing the ends of the kayak to pivot up and down lightly, the different weight distribution in a double, with the weight closer to each end, makes the kayak lift and slam, losing a lot of speed with each slam down.

3 A loaded double is very heavy and several people will be needed to help with any lifting. Your choice of landing and launching sites will be more limited than with a single and will need to be made with extra care.

4 Leaders of groups must decide whether they need to share a kayak with another leader in order to cope efficiently with any emergencies, or with a less experienced paddler in order to add to their paddling speed. In a situation such as a deep-water rescue in adverse conditions, it may be a hindrance to be sharing with an inexperienced paddler.

Collapsible sea kayaks

Sea kayaks generally range from 4.6–5.5 m (15–18 ft) for singles, and up to 7.6 m (25 ft) for doubles. For some people the length presents storage and carriage problems. Rubberized canvas folding kayaks have been available for many years. Lindemann crossed the Atlantic in one in 1956. The whole kayak when disassembled packs away into a couple of cases, and is re-assembled by fitting together a series of struts and rods into the skin. This type of construction is best suited to more sheltered landings as the skin is vulnerable to damage on rocky shores in rough weather.

Inflatable kayaks are available. They combine lightness with surprising strength, but do not

Below *A double kayak in two sections that bolt together is easier to transport.*

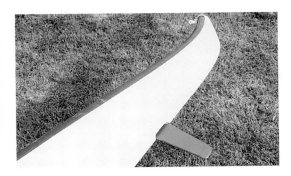

When the retractable skeg is fully down (left) you turn downwind. When it's partly retracted

(right) the kayak lies across the wind. When it's fully retracted you turn into the wind.

have much storage space. They draw little water and so are less controlable in windy conditions.

Glass-reinforced plastic (GRP) kayaks can be made in two or three sections which you take apart and bolt together, making transport, and air transport in particular, a lot easier. Although these are not standard, a number of manufacturers make them to order. I can remember having my sea kayak sawn in half to make it fit into a plane, and sticking it back together with glass fibre on my arrival. This drastic measure isn't necessary nowadays!

Rudders and skegs

A rudder or skeg can be a useful addition to help control a sea kayak that suffers from a lack of directional stability. A permanent skeg may be moulded under the stern of a kayak, but this is vulnerable to damage while launching and landing, as is a removable skeg that is slipped over

the stern of a kayak when needed. Far better is a skeg which is retractable into the hull of the kayak. This can be positioned far enough forward to grip the water even when waves lift the stern clear, but the disadvantage is that valuable storage space is lost, and the 'box' inside the stern makes loading more awkward. The skeg is retracted when not needed, and dropped as necessary to keep the kayak on course. In windy conditions, if the kayak naturally turns upwind, the skeg partly down enables the kayak to be paddled across the wind, and with the skeg dropped further, the kayak will turn downwind. If control is easier, there is a penalty to pay. The skeg will create some drag, slowing you down. Excessive amount of skeg in the water when surfing on a following sea can create sudden instability, caused by the skeg 'planing' to the surface. Retractable skegs sometimes jam with small pebbles, so it is important that you learn to handle your kayak without the skeg so that

It is important to be able to raise the rudder, to avoid damage during launching and landing.

you will not get into difficulties when it jams. The operating mechanism varies from a lifting line and cleat, brought forward to the cockpit, with shock-cord elastic to hold the skeg down, to stainless steel cables which are used to both raise and lower the skeg. If you have a retractable skeg, find out how to dismantle it, and carry a basic repair kit with the necessary tools to effect repairs. However, retractable skegs can be a real asset.

Rudders that can be lifted clear of the water to lie along the stern deck are far superior to arrangements where the rudder blade is permanently in a vulnerable position. This helps avoid damage during launching and landing; the extra drag of the rudder blade is avoided if the rudder is not needed, and you can remove the blade from the water should there be damage to the system. I recommend a rudder where the blade is lifted by means of a line leading to the cockpit, and the rudder can be rigged to be held down by shock-cord elastic so that it will rise if it inadvertently touches against the bottom. Steering is by means of a short tiller between the feet, a dual pedal system or by means of a butterfly bar above the footrest.

Buoyancy, hatches and bulkheads

Sea kayaks need to be fitted with sufficient buoyancy to ensure swift and easy emptying. The most popular way of achieving this is by means of sealed compartments divided by watertight *bulkheads*. These are usually made of GRP or polyethylene foam. The ideal place for them is immediately behind the seat and just beyond the footrest, and in doubles you will need to treat each cockpit in the same way, with a bulkhead at each end of each cockpit. Access to the chambers is normally by means of watertight *hatches* which are positioned in most cases on the deck, and provide dry storage space for equipment. Another good alternative is a system of cockpit-style rim and spray-cover; a system which I have used successfully since 1975. To get a really good seal the hatch needs to be circular and not too large. A separate rigid cover can be used to insure against implosion, although with my own hatches I have never had a case of this.

It is wise to attach your hatch lids to the kayak with a tape or line to prevent loss. I have heard some epic tales resulting from the loss of lids at sea, which could easily have been prevented.

Hatches may be circular (left) or oval (centre). The Vyneck (left) has a second stern hatch offset to permit access at sea. The circular Vyneck rim and neoprene desk hatch (right) works efficiently with an 11-inch diameter, but larger neoprene hatch lids need a rigid top cover to prevent implosion.

Pods and flexible '*socks*' are two other ways of providing buoyancy. The pod, pioneered by Alan Byde, is a very sound idea. A separate chamber is fitted, which becomes the cockpit, which cuts down the space for the paddler to a reasonable minimum. The idea is to so reduce the space that even when the cockpit is awash, the kayak is still perfectly manageable and the stability is little affected. The flexible 'sock' works on the same principle, although there is more scope for failure of the fabric through abrasion, causing leakage into the storage space.

Whichever system is adopted, a common-sense rule should be applied: always fill empty storage spaces with air bags or alternative buoyancy in case of damage to the kayak or hatches. Dealing with a kayak with waterlogged storage compartments in a choppy sea is tricky.

A portable stirrup pump is probably the cheapest pump available but is not the most convenient.

The pump

A pump is standard equipment nowadays. A stirrup pump, which may be passed from kayak to kayak is probably the cheapest. However, you need both hands to operate it and you have to remove the spray-deck to gain access to the cockpit.

You need only one hand to operate a deck-mounted pump; with your free hand you can hold onto another kayak or the paddles for balance. Deck pumps are best mounted on the foredeck so that their housing inside the craft is approximately level with your shins. In this position it will not interfere with your paddling but you need to be careful getting in and out of the cockpit. A removable pump handle is secured to the deck on a length of line.

You may prefer a footpump, which lets you pump and paddle at the same time. Footpumps are mounted on the footrest system. The most effective is fastened to a full-plate footrest, into which the pump is recessed. The footrest is adjusted to your leg length, and the pump follows suit. Pumps can be custom fitted to a fixed bulkhead in a similar way, although maintenance is more difficult. Low volume pumps, such as the excellent Lendal footpump, are used primarily for keeping the kayak dry during paddling, whereas the high volume pumps are more suitable for major emptying, such as draining a kayak following a capsize.

Electric pumps, while they work, are excellent. However, they are not often as reliable as the manual kind. Both hands are free while the pump

A footpump (left) and a hand-operated pump that is mounted on the foredeck.

The low volume Lendal footpump is suitable for keeping the kayak dry during paddling.

Above *A foredeck mounted pump is used to pump dry a kayak after a capsize.*

empties, and the system can be rigged to start automatically when a prescribed water level is reached.

Pumps used to be mounted on the stern deck immediately behind and to one side of the paddler. This is an uncomfortable position for operation, although it is within reach of another paddler. This position leads to the rear bulkhead being placed too far back, making rescues more difficult.

Deck-lines

Deck-lines help you handle the kayak on water and on land, particularly during tricky launches and landings. The lines should be slack enough to let you slip your hand underneath easily yet taut enough for you to gain immediate control of the kayak. They should be fastened at regular intervals to prevent all the slack gathering in one place. The fastening points should be strong enough to support the whole weight of a laden kayak as it is manoeuvred up a rocky shore.

Toggles at bow and stern can help if you capsize and can double as carrying handles. To stop them rattling against the hull while you're paddling, secure them back to the deck with a length of thin shock-cord. You can often use elastics to secure the deck equipment such as spare paddles, a container for emergency gear, and compass and chart. Bear in mind, however, that elastics will not always hold items against the power of surf waves or overfalls, and that many a section of chart and spare paddle has found a watery grave!

Deck-lines and elastics will not last for ever. Check them frequently for signs of wear and replace them regularly.

The compass

This is an essential piece of equipment for the sea paddler. Its simplest use is to lead you to safety if fog develops, providing of course that you know in which direction land lies. At its most sophisticated it can be used for navigating wider stretches of water to islands in varying visibility. For emergency purposes, a simple orienteering compass is perfectly adequate. Make

A compass mounted onto the front deck hatch can be read without dropping your eyes far from the horizon.

sure however that it is *fluid-filled* as an air-filled compass will let in water and rapidly corrode and become useless. For more pre-planned navigational purposes I would recommend a much larger compass mounted further away from you on the front deck. Although short distances can be paddled with an orienteering compass close to your lap, it is not a relaxing place to look constantly and can lead to seasickness. A compass that can be viewed from the side rather than from above is best, and distancing it from the cockpit allows easy reading without dropping your eyes far from the horizon. A good mounting position is on your front hatch lid, where it can easily be removed for safety when not required. *Remember* that a compass will be affected by metal objects such as cutlery, radios and torches. Store such items, together with tins, away from your compass.

Custom-fitting a kayak

Customizing your sea kayak is a worthwhile exercise. Let us start with the cockpit. Paddle the kayak to see how comfortable it is. Try a few support and recovery strokes and maybe a roll or two. You will soon get an idea of how well you fit. If necessary, pad out your seat to the sides to prevent excessive sideways movement when your kayak goes out of balance. If you find you do not have sufficient grip for your knees, then a *knee tube* may solve your problem. This is a tube or half tube fitted to the underside of the deck,

providing both knee control and a useful storage space accessible as soon as you remove your spray-deck. Knee tubes may restrict you a little, getting in and out of the cockpit. Padding on the outside of the tube will add comfort. Knee tubes can be fitted purely for storage, in which case they can be fitted to allow you to bring your knees together without interference.

Now for your back. A back-strap is an advantage. It should support the back low down so as not to hinder trunk rotation. A back-strap that

You will find it well worth your while to fit a supportive back-strap.

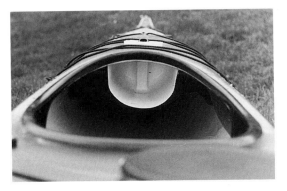

A knee tube can fulfill a dual purpose, giving knee control and an accessible storage space.

is too tight, making the space between the foot-rest and your back-strap too short, even by a fraction, will be excruciatingly uncomfortable. Be warned! One way of fitting a back-strap is to fasten it to the side supports of the seat on either side, with an additional strap anchored to the deck just inside the rear of your cockpit, ensuring that the back-strap cannot slip down. Another way of making a backrest is to shape a block of closed-cell foam to fit against the rear bulkhead which, incidentally, cuts down on excess space in the cockpit.

Footrests can often be improved or upgraded. Full-plate or bulkhead footrests are undoubtedly the most comfortable to use, as they permit the maximum possible variety of foot positions during paddling. They may be padded with foam for warmth and comfort. A well positioned bulkhead will maximize your stowage space and provide a secure footrest. If you do have your front bulk-head positioned for this purpose, always leave a little extra space and then pad it out to the correct fit. The Vyneck I used to circumnavigate Iceland in 1977 had a perfectly positioned bulkhead for a footrest, but when I used it for an expedition to Newfoundland the following year I wore different footwear and found myself in extreme discomfort. I was forced to remove my footwear for paddling simply because the soles were slightly thicker. Padding can be removed or added far more easily than moving a bulkhead.

Paddle park

A paddle park is a device to secure your paddle when it is not in your hand. It can be useful when you are involved in a rescue, or using your hands for other purposes. A simple arrangement is to take a short length of strong shock-cord elastic, fasten one end to your deck near your cockpit or onto your buoyancy aid and fasten a small clip to the other end. When the elastic is looped around the paddle shaft and the clip fastened back onto the elastic again, the noose will keep your paddle captive until you need it again. The elastic need not be very long to allow you to start paddling without removing the paddle park, should this be necessary.

Colour

The choice of colour for a sea kayak is very much a matter of personal taste. However, certain colours are much more visible at sea, and a major school of thought is that your kayak should be easily seen for rescue purposes. The colours through the red, orange and yellow part of the spectrum are considered the most visible, al-though perhaps surprisingly, black and white show up well. Black is very good when you are looking into light, and white especially good when the light is shining on it, and in low light. Translucent kayaks and the colours green and dark blue show up poorly. I have a friend in Denmark who paddles a dull green kayak to avoid being spotted while bird-watching . . . not by birds, which do not seem to mind a bit of colour, but by people who might mistake his intentions! Incidentally, if you are watching out for kayakers, it is usually the paddle blades that attract the attention first because of the flashing movement. White, again, seems to be par-ticularly visible.

Weight and strength

Weight is another personal decision. The intro-duction of diolen, kevlar, carbon fibre and core-mat as strengtheners and stiffeners has meant that sea kayaks can be made very light, strong and rigid – for a price. Otherwise, made from the same materials, a light kayak has less strength than a heavy one, so decide how much rough handling yours is going to get.

For solo paddling a lightweight kayak is a must, and you must treat it with care.

For expedition work the handling of the kayak must be considered. Handling will be improved by allowing more freeboard, which is done by cutting down on weight. A saving of 13.5 kg (30 lb) in the weight of the kayak can allow you 13.5 kg (30 lb) more luggage weight with no loss of freeboard.

I would consider 28–30 kg (62–6 lb) as being a reasonable maximum unladen weight for a single sea kayak when you need to carry it.

Doubles

For safety, doubles should be fitted with at least one bulkhead between the two paddlers in addi-tion to one fore and aft. Two or more central bulkheads create a buoyancy or storage chamber in a part of the kayak that has a high volume, greatly helping rescues. Each cockpit should be fitted with its own pump and customized as neces-sary. It is normal for the rear paddler to have control of the rudder if fitted, although the cables could easily be taken through to the bow. If a rudder is fitted, then the person controlling it must have a view of the compass.

Buoyancy aid or personal flotation device

A buoyancy aid is an essential part of the kayaker's clothing. The most common is the waistcoat shape which fastens at the front. This is easier to remove than one that you pull on over your head, so you can adjust the clothing underneath while at sea. The buoyancy usually comes from closed-cell foam, although air sacs are sometimes used. There should be a minimum of 6 kg (13 lb) of buoyancy.

A lifejacket is the alternative. Lifejackets for kayaking usually have a minimum of 6 kg (13 lb) of inherent buoyancy positioned at the chest and behind the neck, with the capacity for inflation to 16 kg (35 lb) either by CO_2 cylinder or orally. This has the advantage of turning the wearer into a face-up position should he be incapacitated. A lifejacket is a wise choice for paddling open crossings of any great length. Some paddlers wear a lifejacket with no inherent buoyancy over their standard buoyancy aid. This can be inflated if needed, but the paddler still has the comfort and protection of his standard buoyancy aid in the meantime.

Personally, I find pockets on a buoyancy aid almost indispensable for keeping handy items such as a small compass, flares, emergency repair tape, a couple of plasters for thumbs and a chocolate bar or two. Pockets are rarely completely waterproof, so a good alternative is to have pockets which drain readily. If your buoyancy aid includes an integral tow-line system and a fold-away hood, you will always have these items to hand when you need them, whatever else you are wearing at the time.

In Britain, look for the approval label of either the BCU/BCMA or of the British Marine Industries Federation (BMIF) as a guide to the satisfactory quality of a buoyancy aid.

Paddles

There are several different schools of thought about the type of paddle most suitable for sea kayaking.

Most major expeditions from Britain are carried out using asymmetric and feathered paddles. These have a clean entry and exit from the water and grip the water well from the start of the paddle stroke. The paddle rate depends on the length of the shaft: a shorter shaft increases the paddle rate, while a longer shaft slows it down. Many manufacturers produce narrower asymmetric blades for use with the longer shafts, as otherwise these become quite hard to use. Long paddles give greater turning leverage but are more difficult to use close to the kayak, which makes it harder to go straight. However, kayaks

A double-torque paddle shaft with asymmetric blades combines a comfortable hand position with efficiency in use.

with a broad beam require slightly longer paddles than narrow kayaks.

Shorter paddles are less demanding on tendons and muscles, requiring a greater number of revolutions instead, and allowing greater acceleration. I find a broad-bladed asymmetric paddle of about 216 cm (7 ft 1 in or 85 in) overall length suits most of my sea paddling. I find longer paddles a strain with loaded sea kayaks, making it difficult for me to accelerate to catch following waves. I find shorter paddles bring my stroke rate with unladen kayaks to an unreasonably high rate. I can handle 216 cm (7 ft 1 in or 85 in) paddles easily, even in gale force winds. I am 6 ft tall, and my paddles reach to the top of my wrist if I stand with my arm upstretched beside my paddle.

Asymmetric paddles are usually feathered at about 65–85°, since a feathering of less than 90° causes fewer wrist problems. Double-torque or cranked shafts give a more comfortable hand position which is also likely to reduce possible wrist problems, and they also lead to the better use of paddling muscles. I believe they will come into widespread use for sea kayaking.

Some enthusiasts advocate the use of traditional Inuit narrow-bladed paddles. They argue that the length and narrowness of the blade permit a range of stroke rates according to the amount of blade dipped into the water with each stroke. They are clearly not so good for acceleration, but this is not considered important for all types of sea kayaking. There are two main

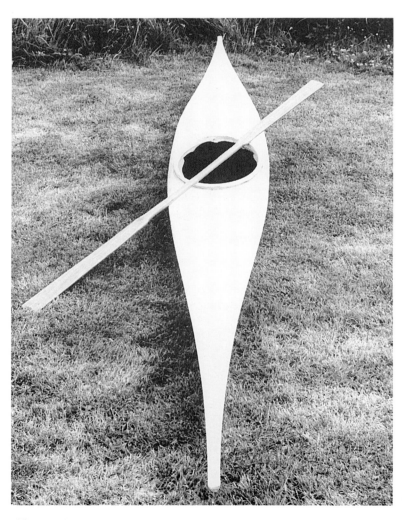

A copy of an East Greenland kayak and paddle.

types of narrow-bladed paddle: a short paddle of perhaps 160–5 cm (63–5 in), and a longer one of maybe 230 cm (90½ in), of which each blade is about 78 cm (31 in) long and 10 cm (4 in) wide. Historically, the short style was used in stronger winds when the paddle would be caught less by the wind than the longer paddles. The hands are moved towards the end of the paddle for each paddle stroke, thus allowing a normal paddling rate to be maintained. This type of paddle is not feathered, although it would be possible to feather the longer style. The blades are flat, so do not give such an efficient grip on the water. This type of paddle favours a slower paddling pace.

Incidentally, wing paddles developed for racing have been used successfully for distance paddling in calm conditions.

Spare paddles carried as splits should match as far as possible the type of paddle you normally use, both in style and length. For expeditions involving freighting your equipment, you might consider using only split paddles, as they can be carried inside your kayak for safety.

Paddle flutter

Paddle flutter is most uncomfortable. This is the 'falling leaf' movement of the blade from side to side as you pull on it, and makes you grip the shaft harder, hurting your wrists. A longitudinal central spine along the face of the blade helps to cure the problem, which is worst when a paddle is drawn rapidly through the water. The longer the paddle, the more likely it is to flutter. Also a more flexible blade will flutter under lower power than a rigid one. Carbon fibre stiffened blades on a reasonably short shaft give a combination that almost eradicates flutter even when you are accelerating fast. Another 'cure' is to paddle more slowly.

Whereas it is desirable to have a stiff blade, very rigid paddle shafts can lead to jarring, and pain in your hands, especially when broad blades are used. A more flexible shaft, giving just a little 'spring', is much more forgiving.

Clothing

Sea kayaking in cold weather requires special clothing. You might wear a wetsuit long-john, sweater, waterproof cagoule and wetsuit boots. Alternatively, try a fibre-pile or woollen top and trousers beneath salopettes and cagoule, worn with rubber sailing boots. A third option for your

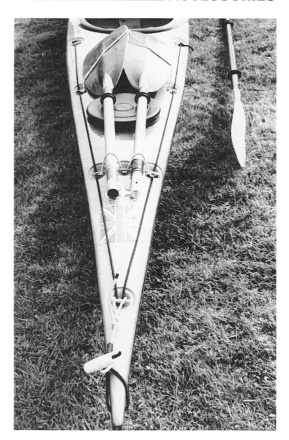

Any group of sea kayakers should carry at least one spare paddle. This is essential equipment, which may be stored on the rear deck.

outer layer is a one- or two-piece drysuit, with latex wrist, neck and ankle seals. This gives the greatest protection from the water. A woollen hat and windproof pogies (gauntlets that fasten around the paddle shaft to protect your hands while still letting you grip the shaft) can complete your protection, not forgetting your buoyancy aid and spray-deck.

A useful item of spare clothing is a hooded anorak large enough for you to pull on over your buoyancy aid as an additional layer. Pockets on anoraks and buoyancy aids are useful for carrying items you want handy, but beware of overloading them with weighty items.

In hot weather a light cotton shirt with long sleeves, and a peaked hat will help prevent sunburn, and sun-glasses can protect your eyes against the sun's glare.

Spray-decks

These can be of neoprene, latex rubber, or waterproofed nylon, but they must be in good condition. A leaky spray-deck will allow your cockpit to fill up surprisingly quickly. The waist seal needs to be firm around your waist, or held up by a shoulder strap. Fabric should be taut to stop water pooling. It is essential that your spray-deck does not cave in under the pressure of the waves. For longer expeditions a spare spray-deck is essential.

Care of your equipment

Always wash your sea kayaking clothing after use, in fresh water if possible, otherwise salt will crystallize between the fibres of the fabric and accelerate the wearing out of the fibres. On expeditions, if you have no access to fresh water for this, and your gear is accumulating salt, then a rinse in seawater will reduce the amount of crystal salt.

Above *In rough conditions a good helmet will help protect your head.*

The well-dressed sea kayaker is wearing here high waisted overtrousers, a cagoule and a twin-seal spray-deck. His buoyancy aid features an integral hood, draining pockets and reflective tape for visibility at night.

Pogies – windproof gauntlets – protect your hands but do not interfere with your grip on the shaft.

A well-prepared sea paddler carries enough equipment to cope with most situations, believing it is better to practise self-sufficiency on the water rather than call for outside help. To help you decide what equipment to carry, let's look at a number of situations that occur on the sea and what you will need to deal with them.

1. Someone in your group damages his kayak, but only discovers the leak when committed to an area where landing is not possible.
Even a small hole will let in water faster than you can pump it out. An accessible repair kit is needed, and the means to repair a wet boat. Waterproof duct tape and plumbers mastic tape will both stick to wet surfaces, and taping on a stout polyethylene patch will support a larger hole. A more comprehensive repair kit, containing needle and thread, fabric and glue for patching garments, and non-mastic cloth-backed tape for dry repairs to hulls or paddles may be carried in the kayak.

Plumbers' mastic tape is messy to use. I cut sections from the roll, peel off the backing film and stick them to a strip of heavy gauge polyethylene ready for use. The patches are sealed in a polythene bag along with further polythene bags to protect my hands while applying patches; otherwise the mastic lingers on my paddles for days! This basic repair kit lives in the pocket of my buoyancy aid.

2. Someone in your group becomes ill or injured while on the water, and is unable to continue paddling. Or someone becomes too tired to make it to the shore.
A tow-line should be carried by every sea paddler, and kept handy. Attach it to your rear deck by means of a quick-release cleat, or around your waist by means of a quick-release waist belt. The quick-release may be a buckle or velcro. 6 mm (¼ in) braided polypropylene line is suitable. Your whole system should float.

The clip used for attaching the rope to the other boat should be fairly large for ease of use; if it is large enough to use with mittened hands it is suitable for use with cold hands. It should be long enough to allow a kayak length between the boats. Longer tow-lines are vital in a following sea, otherwise the towed craft will catch up with you each time it picks up a wave. Tow-lines can

be joined together for extra length. The towing point needs to be near the cockpit of the towing craft, not through the end loop at the stern as this can make steering extremely difficult.

However, beware of your line catching around any gear on your stern deck, or the hatch lids, which can lift off during towing. An elastic insert, with the tow-line wound around the shock-cord for neatness, will take much of the jerking out of towing. The line must be continuous however, and arranged so that the elastic cannot be over-stretched.

3. Someone needs first aid.
A basic first aid kit can be carried in a handy pocket, consisting of plasters and adhesive tape for binding sore thumbs before they blister, and seasickness tablets. A more comprehensive first aid kit is best stored in your kayak, in an accessible place.

Basic first aid kit

a triangular bandage
Melolin gauze dressing (for burns)
crepe bandage
plasters
adhesive tape
scissors
tweezers
headache tablets
pencil and paper
matches or lighter
a small pair of pliers (for such emergencies as
    cutting and extracting fish hooks)
eye bath
petroleum jelly (to prevent excessive drying
    of skin)
anti-seasickness wrist bands
sterile strips/sutures (for open wounds)

---

4. One paddler becomes separated from the rest.
A whistle, compass and waterproof chart should be carried by each paddler. Make sure everyone knows how to use them.

5. Somebody shows signs of the early stages of hypothermia.
You should be able to lay your hands on some additional warm clothing, an exposure bag, a

hot drink and some emergency food without too much difficulty. Prevention, if the problem is anticipated in time, is easier than a cure later.

6. You cannot deal with an emergency, and need to call on outside assistance.
Attract attention using radio, distress flares or some other internationally recognized distress signal such as the raising and lowering of both arms. *There are no guarantees.* Your signal may fail to attract attention, or help may not arrive for some considerable time. Be cautious and try not to operate near the limits of your ability if the results of a mistake might require the help of an outside agency. If you are in the water and appear likely to remain there for some time, get into an exposure bag to help keep you warm. An inflated exposure bag will make you more easily spotted. Clip yourself to your kayak with your tow-line to prevent separation, as your kayak is more visible than you are. Always try to reserve at least one distress flare for a time when rescuers

Left *A well-prepared sea paddler believes it is better to practise self-sufficiency on the water than call for outside help.*

Below *Getting into an exposure bag helps conserve your body's heat in the water.*

To attract attention after a capsize you can use the slightest of breezes to inflate an exposure bag. Gather it at the neck and it will make you more easily spotted.

are searching nearby. Keep your flares as dry as possible, and at least one on your person. Parachute flares which float down from a height of about 330 m (1000 ft) are particularly effective for offshore paddling (more than 13 km (8 miles) offshore) and for beneath cliffs of less than 330 m (1000 ft). Orange smoke flares and miniflares may be sufficient within a shorter range, and are excellent as markers when rescuers are searching, while red pinpoint hand-held flares do the same job at night. Whatever attention-seeking devices you carry, make sure that you know where you have stored them and how to operate them. They should be handy, but secure.

Chapter 6 describes some self-rescue techniques that can help you help yourself.

Essential equipment
chart and compass
repair kit
first aid kit
whistle
flares/distress signals
tow-line
spare clothing
emergency food and hot drink
exposure bag
spare paddles

7. Someone damages or loses his paddle.
Each group on the water should carry *at least* one spare paddle. These are normally jointed in the centre for ease of carrying. Make sure that each section floats: I have seen some hollow-shafted split paddles sink. I have rarely needed to use spare paddles, but on one occasion two sets of paddles were broken within half an hour.

4 Launching and landing

Launching and landing can be simplicity itself, but sometimes it is the most difficult and dangerous part of a journey. Choose your launching site with care. Try to find a low rock so you can float your kayak beside it and climb in without even getting your feet wet. Alternatively, seal launch from a gently shelving beach onto calm water. Watch out for rough water and steeply shelving beaches or rocks.

Launching from a surf beach

Study of a surf beach will normally reveal a rip, which is an outward flowing stream of water in which the wave pattern is broken. Rips are normally found at the ends of a beach, but may be found at intervals along the length of a beach, and wherever a stream or river crosses the beach. Rips are caused by the escape of white water ('soup') that has built up on the shore. The resulting current can attain a rate of several knots and can give you valuable assistance when paddling out through surf.

A seal launch is the easiest way afloat, although you may need assistance to keep your kayak straight until it is fully afloat. Paddle out during a lull (see Chapter 12) and time your paddle strokes so that you reach over each broken wave to plant your paddle beyond it, pulling yourself through the waves. Determined paddling is needed to stop yourself being pushed back towards the beach. When paddling out through steep waves at speed, you will find your kayak almost takes off at the crests before plunging sharply into the troughs. This can upset your balance, so perform a low brace to steady yourself as you land. Finally, wait for the rest of the group well beyond the break line.

Rolling under waves

Sometimes the simplest option when you meet a big collapsing surf wave is to roll beneath the water to allow the wave to pass along your up-turned hull, and roll upright again when the wave has passed. In this way, you can usually avoid a fast backward run towards the beach, or the possibility of a back-loop.

Below *Preparing for a seal launch (photo: Mark Harrison).*

Rolling under the waves

Capsize as the wave approaches. Wait for the turbulence to subside before rolling up again. This can save a lot of energy in powerful surf.

Above *When launching from a surf beach, determined paddling is needed to break through the waves.*

Below *To make a controlled landing on a surf beach you can reverse to 'stall' the kayak and stop it being surfed forward.*

Landing on a surf beach

Landing through surf can be an intimidating prospect. It is essential that you choose your beach with care to avoid powerful dumpers. Pick a lull and paddle quickly towards the shore, reversing whenever there is a possibility that you may be surfed forwards on a wave. In this

way you can avoid being swept in sideways, and you will have enough control to avoid bathers and to be able to change your mind if the final landing appears unsafe. Time your approach so the wave breaks in front of you, then paddle in on its back. Climb out smartly and quickly haul your kayak clear of the danger zone.

Dumpers

A dumper is a wave that breaks powerfully onto a steeply shelving beach. Avoid them if at all possible; I have seen sea kayaks split by quite small dumpers, and their explosive power is deceptive.

If there is no choice, send the most able paddler in first, with a throw-line made up of several tow-lines. The team then paddles in as for surf, on the backs of the waves, while the first paddler provides safety cover with the throw-line.

If you capsize in a dumper, get well clear of your kayak quickly as a wave-thrown sea kayak can do you a lot of damage.

Launching from a steep shore

If the sea is calm, first float your kayak, then climb aboard. However, in rougher conditions,

Above *Landing onto steep rock can be tricky. Here a more experienced sea kayaker gives assistance.*

try a seal launch. Watch out for the moment when your bow is supported by the water but your stern is still in contact with the beach, and carry out a low brace on one side to prevent a capsize.

Seal-launching from rock carries the same risk, plus the possibility of the bow jamming if you have not checked the water depth! Try to choose rock that is free from barnacles and sharp edges that might gouge your hull, or choose one that is well covered with seaweed. Alternatively, position pieces of driftwood to protect your kayak.

As a last resort it is possible to manhandle your kayaks onto the water, swim them clear, and help each other into the cockpits.

Rafted landing onto steep rock

Landing onto steep rock, especially when there is a swell running, can be difficult to manage unaided. Providing the rock is sufficiently steep,

Launching from a steep shore

First float your kayak. Make sure that your paddle remains within your reach while you climb aboard.

Seal launching from seaweed covered rock.

Launching from a steep shore

Get into your kayak close to the water. Use your hands to shuffle down the beach. There is a moment of instability when both ends are supported but not the cockpit region. Support yourself with a low brace until you are completely afloat. In the

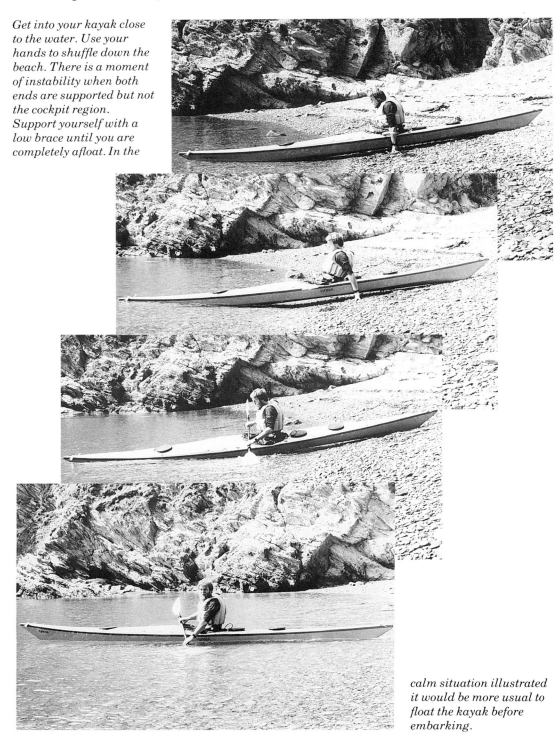

calm situation illustrated it would be more usual to float the kayak before embarking.

that it drops steeply into water deep enough to prevent the swell from breaking, and that it has suitable handholds, the most straightforward method is a rafted landing. Two kayaks raft together, with the paddler in the kayak nearer the rock steadying the raft and keeping it close to but not touching the rock, while the paddler in the outermost kayak steps across onto the rock and climbs clear. Further paddlers can be landed before kayaks are manoeuvred ashore at a suitable site. If conditions are difficult, it may sometimes be necessary for the final paddler to get into the water before being helped ashore.

Launching and landing doubles

Doubles are more cumbersome to launch and land than singles. When launching from a beach float the bow and have one person hold the boat while the bow man gets in. The stern paddler then pushes the boat forward and gets in while the bow paddler keeps the kayak pointing into the waves. Landing is similar.

A careful study of your chart or map will often reveal landing places that are easier than the more obvious ones. Go for the sheltered side of a headland, coastline protected by an island or a beach sheltered by a sandbar. Indented coastlines frequently have tiny coves where the sea laps gently onto the shore, while a short distance away the surf pounds heavily onto the beach. (See Chapter 12 for wave refraction.)

In a double, the rear paddler steadies the kayak and points it into oncoming waves while the bow paddler embarks. Then the bow paddler keeps the kayak pointing into the waves and away from the shore while the rear paddler embarks.

5 Turning

One of the most important skills to perfect is turning. Except for very short, stable sea kayaks, most sea kayaks do not turn easily with sweep strokes when upright. However, turning is much easier when they are tilted or leaned over.

Tilted turns

To alter course to the left while paddling forwards, tilt your kayak to the right and perform a forward sweep stroke on the right using a slightly angled blade (to give you extra stability). Straighten your right leg, raise your left knee

against the inside of the deck and hold your body as upright as possible to maintain balance. The kayak should be held at a tilt throughout the turn, while your paddle either alternates between forward strokes on the left and forward sweep strokes on the right, or performs repeated sweeps on the right, returning the blade to the bow each time by skimming it forwards in a low brace position so that you can use it for support should you begin to lose balance. The tilt brings a more manoeuvrable part of the hull into contact with the water, and the paddle sweep is performed on the side towards which you tilt so as to aid stability.

Leaned turns

Leaned turns

Whereas a tilted turn angles the kayak as far as possible without tipping it off balance, the leaned turn puts it well over onto its side to a point where your balance can only be maintained with the help of your paddle. Build up forward speed, then throw the kayak over onto the side towards which you want to turn. Carry out a reverse sweep with the paddle blade angled to provide the power for the turn, while the curvature of the side of the kayak becomes the effective rocker. Carry the sweep forwards only as far as a point level with the cockpit. A good leaned turn will turn most sea kayaks through 90° in one stroke, but steep-sided hulls will be more stable in this position than round-sided ones.

Leaned and tilted turns need practice and a degree of confidence. Practise whenever you can in safe rough water so that you are not deterred when the need to turn quickly arises.

Rudders are often fitted by people who do not have the confidence to tilt or lean turn, but I consider them an additional way of turning rather than a substitute as they often fail.

Turning doubles

Doubles in which the cockpits lie to either side of the centre point tend to turn surprisingly easily while held upright by the use of sweep strokes; carry out forward sweeps from the bow to a point level with the cockpit and reverse sweeps from the stern to a point level with the rear cockpit. Doubles may be tilt-turned in the same way as singles. The bow paddler again sweeps only in an arc forward of the cockpit, whereas the stern paddler uses only an arc behind the cockpit for turning. Leaned turns require a lot of coordination between the paddlers, so I recommend you always keep the kayak in balance when tilted, even if you are using strokes to turn.

Extended paddles

Beginners, and frequently more experienced paddlers, sometimes are reluctant to tilt a kayak for turning when conditions become rough. This can make turning slow and difficult. Under such circumstances you can extend your paddle towards one side providing greater leverage and speeding up the turn.

Turning a double. The rear paddler uses a reverse sweep from the stern to the position shown. The bow paddler uses a forward sweep from the bow to the point shown. The kayak turns on the spot.

Opposite In the leaned turn illustrated, note how the water reaches well across the paddler's spray-deck.

6 Rescues

We all capsize sooner or later. Bear the following points in mind when deciding which rescue method to adopt. Rescues are easier in an unladen craft than in one equipped for an expedition. Bulkheads simplify the operation but the shape of your kayak may make rescue more tricky.

Below *The X rescue.*

The X rescue

This is the most straightforward rescue, beyond simply righting the boat and pumping it dry. Approach the upturned kayak and grasp it at the *bow* end. It is essential that the capsized paddler remains in contact with his own or the rescue kayak *at all times* during the rescue procedure. If he doesn't, the kayaks may be blown along faster than he can swim.

Right the inverted kayak, lift the bow across your foredeck, and roll it onto its side. If it doesn't drain completely on its side, roll it upside down to finish the job. Right the kayak, lift it back onto the water and swing it alongside your craft. Direct the stern of the empty boat towards your bow: the person in the water will find it easiest to get back in from that direction. Rest both paddles across both decks and grip the empty kayak at the front of the cockpit. Direct the swimmer to come between the two kayaks to hold the back of their cockpit with one hand and your deck with their other hand. By lying back into the water, lifting both their feet into their cockpit, and pulling the two kayaks together behind them, they can re-enter. You will need to steady their kayak until their spray-deck is secure. Separating again can sometimes be an awkward manoeuvre, especially with tippy kayaks on choppy water. Instruct your companion to perform a low brace support on the water while you push their kayak firmly past you. The movement lends stability to the paddle brace until the kayaks are far enough apart for normal paddling.

Doubles rescue

The simplest doubles rescue is really a form of self-rescue. This will only be quick and effective if the kayak is fitted as follows. There should be a bulkhead immediately behind the seat and a short way beyond the feet of each paddler. If the cockpits are broad, then the inside space can be narrowed by fixing buoyancy to either side. Finally, both cockpits should be provided with pumps.

Following a capsize, the kayak is righted and one swimmer steadies the kayak while the other climbs aboard from the opposite side and secures their spray-deck. The other swimmer climbs aboard while the first steadies the kayak with a support stroke. 'Stirrups' make easier both steadying the kayak and climbing aboard. Both paddlers can then pump dry together, or one may paddle while the other bails. If the kayak is too unsteady with both paddlers aboard before bailing, then it would be worth reducing the inside volume of the cockpits. In the meantime, perform the rescue as described, but pump the first cockpit dry before the second paddler re-enters.

The H rescue

This rescue is not as straightforward as the previous one, but can be used to empty double kayaks that are not so well fitted with bulkheads.

Roll the up-turned kayak onto its side and

Above *An X rescue performed with two double kayaks.*

slowly draw it up the decks of the two rescue kayaks in an H formation. The water drains out as the rescue kayaks pull closer together. To drain it completely, turn it upside down and lift the bow. Alternatively, right it on the water and let the paddler(s) pump out any remaining water after they have got back in.

The Ipswich rescue

This makes use of two rescue craft, rafted together on either side of the capsized kayak. The rescuers hold their paddles between their shoulders, keeping them firmly in place with their inside hands. With their outer hands they lift the bow of the upturned kayak using deck-lines on either side to keep it level. The swimmer may assist by holding the ends of the kayaks together. Once the water has drained from the cockpit, the rescuers right the craft and place it on the water between them. The swimmer returns to their cockpit. The rescue needs coordination between the rescuers, and cannot be started until both are in position, so it is often slower than an X rescue. However, it is stable and effective, and does not place any strain on the foredeck.

Self-rescue in a double kayak

Anchored rescues

It is often preferable to 'anchor' a rescue to prevent the party drifting downwind. This is essential if there are dangerous rocks downwind. A paddler not involved with the actual rescue attaches a tow-line to the stern of the rescuer's kayak and paddles into the wind or away from the danger. The paddler checks the drift rather than making much progress, until the capsize victim is out of the water. As a self-help procedure, the swimmer should swim his kayak away from danger, or into the wind, while awaiting a rescue and while it is in progress.

Self rescues for single kayaks

Self rescues range from a quick time-saver following a beginner's capsize in straightforward conditions, to advanced techniques to be used when things are going badly. At its simplest, a paddler may re-enter his kayak by first pressing down the stern, which raises the bow and drains much of the water from the cockpit. Then he flips the kayak upright and re-enters by hauling himself across it, swinging one leg across to sit astride close behind the cockpit, then sliding into the

Above In an anchored rescue, the rescuer is held away from the rocks by another paddler with a towline.

seat. He then sponges, bails or pumps out the remaining water. The kayak needs to be well-packed with buoyancy or fitted with a pod for this rescue to be really effective, and it needs to be fairly stable.

Using the paddle

The use of a paddle held across the kayak with one blade lying flat in the water, preferably just submerged, increases stability for re-entry. A device known as the 'paddle float' makes the process even easier. This was developed by Will Nordby in California, and resembles an inflatable envelope which is blown up over the paddle blade. The paddle float is at its most effective if it contains both air and water, preventing it from rising easily from the sea. It can also be used to assist in a re-entry and roll.

Opposite *Self-rescue using a paddle float.*

Self-rescue using 'paddle tubes'

A split paddle, secure in its paddle tube, angled downwards.

Following a similar line of thought, Howard Jeffs of North Wales developed the ingenious 'paddle tubes' method of stabilizing a kayak. Tubes incorporated into the sides of the kayak angle upwards towards the inside of the deck behind the paddler. Spare paddles are inserted and fastened into these tubes; the blades angling down into the water to either side providing a high degree of stability. Re-entry becomes straightforward. After re-fitting the spray-deck and bailing, the final stage is to remove and stow away the spare paddles. This is the most difficult move in the whole process and the one which needs the most practice. Paddling with the split paddles in position is not practical because of the high drag.

Towing

Tow-lines are described in Chapter 3. They are important safety aids and their use should be practised. You can use them to help a paddler experiencing difficulty in directional control, or simply someone who is tired. If the conditions are getting rougher, use a towrope to prevent a capsize, by rafting two kayaks together for towing. This may increase the speed and/or the overall safety of a group. In other more serious circumstances, they may be used to evacuate a

Opposite *Howard Jeffs demonstrates a self-rescue using paddle tubes. Secure your paddles into their tubes to provide a high degree of stability which makes re-entry straightforward.*

casualty, safeguard a rescue, or to tow a capsized paddler to a more sheltered position prior to a deep water rescue.

There are ways of sharing the load of towing. The *tandem tow*, where two or more paddlers attach their tow-lines kayak-to-kayak in line with the victim at the end, adds power and makes steering easier in awkward conditions. Alternatively, use a *fan tow*, where several towing kayaks are more or less in line abreast. If you are towing one kayak, attach the tow-lines to a central point on each of the towing kayaks (so they will be able to steer) and clip them onto the towed kayak's sides near the cockpit.

The fan tow is particularly useful for towing two or more kayaks together to form a stable platform. Use this *rafted tow* if there's any possibility of the person being towed capsizing. If only one kayak is towing, attach the end of each rafted

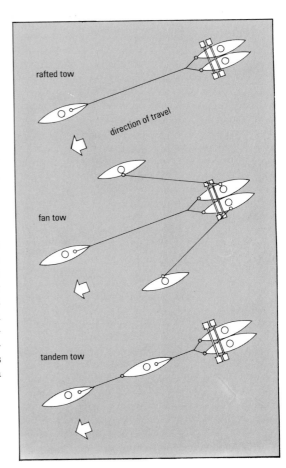

kayak to the tow-line so that they cannot drift apart during towing.

Practise using an *anchor man*, who attaches his tow-line to the kayak of a rescuer to prevent those involved in a deep-water rescue from being carried down-wind. This makes a rescue easier in fact by pointing the rescuer downwind. You can also use an anchor man to prevent towed kayaks from surfing forwards onto the towing kayaks during landings or in steep following seas, although this is a difficult technique requiring skill and practice.

The re-entry and roll

The most effective self rescue in rough conditions in my opinion is the re-entry and roll. Even experienced paddlers occasionally exit from their kayaks, and this is often in circumstances where a conventional rescue may present more danger to bodies and boats than a prolonged swim or a tow out of the danger area. A self rescue can speed up the rescue process.

Hold the kayak by the cockpit and roll it onto its side, with the cockpit open towards the

The re-entry and roll

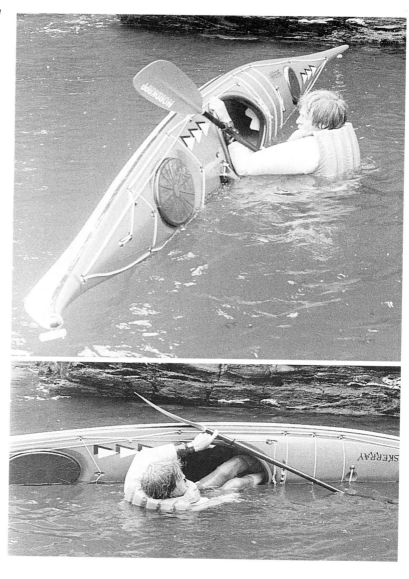

oncoming waves or wind. Grasp the cockpit firmly with your hands either side, and manoeuvre your legs into position in the cockpit. Your body will not normally sink below the surface until you are almost completely seated, when a recovery stroke or roll will right the kayak. An extended paddle roll will increase your confidence and improve the reliability of this manoeuvre, as the kayak will contain some water. You can also use a paddle float, especially for early practice sessions until you are proficient at the re-entry. Once the kayak is upright you may paddle away, although it will be a little tippier than usual. The trickiest stage is replacing your spray-deck in rough conditions, and it is not worth pumping until you have done this. Spray-decks can be replaced once you are out of the immediate danger, or by rafting up. If you add an inflatable lifejacket over your buoyancy aid you can perform a re-entry and roll without your face being submerged. This reduces anxiety, especially when you are learning the technique.

Raft-assisted resuscitation

Raft-assisted resuscitation

Although it may sometimes be necessary to get out of your kayak to support and resuscitate a non-breathing person, resuscitation should be carried out across a raft of kayaks if at all possible. In this way you can continue for longer and you may be able to tow the raft ashore. Roll the patient onto his back and haul him across the kayaks from the side, using either the shoulders of his buoyancy aid or some other convenient grab hold. Alternatively, turn the victim to face the raft and let the paddler in the further kayak haul the victim by his wrists. Once he is clear of the water and in balance, turn him on his back and prepare him for resuscitation. A non-breathing capsize victim can be treated by a single rescuer in a similar way by using the victim's kayak as a roller over which he can be hauled. You should familiarize yourself with current resuscitation techniques and external cardiac compression.

Self help

If you are in the water with your kayak, with an onshore wind and an undesirable shore, swim yourself out to sea with your kayak while you are waiting for another kayak to rescue you, and continue to swim in the same direction while the rescue is in progress to help check the shore-ward drift of the rescue. To free both arms for swimming, attach yourself to your kayak with your tow-line.

Repairs

Repairs may be carried out on kayaks while at sea. If the paddler of the damaged kayak leans across the deck of another kayak, the damaged hull will be revealed to a third paddler who can then locate and place a patch over the damaged area. If there are only two paddlers, the first will either need to scull for support while the repair is effected, or the kayak may be repaired

Opposite and above *You can use your kayaks as a platform for resuscitation.*

Raft-assisted resuscitation

while the victim sits astride the rescuer's kayak. The damaged kayak, if it is not too heavy, may be drawn across the rescuer's kayak to aid stability while this is done.

For safety, an air bag is a useful item of extra equipment for a group leader. It can be used to fill a waterlogged compartment in a kayak if suitable precautions have not already been made to prevent the compartment from filling. Ideally, all empty compartments would be filled with air bags.

Above *You can use a capsized kayak as a roller to bring a victim into position for resuscitation.*

7 The Eskimo roll and Eskimo rescue

Both these techniques are useful rescue procedures. The Eskimo rescue requires outside assistance, and the roll is the perfect self rescue.

The Eskimo rescue

1 The capsized paddler bangs on the bottom of his kayak to attract attention, then leaves one hand on each side of the kayak, extending up into the air.
2 The rescuer approaches from the end of the capsized craft, checking his speed by catching hold of the upturned hull.
3 The rescuer guides his kayak into the reach of the waiting hand. With sea kayaks, it is best to present the side of your kayak, where there are handy deck-lines to grasp.
4 The victim flicks his kayak upright using the rescuer's kayak for support.

An alternative method makes use of the rescuer's paddle as something to pull up on. This is a risky business. If the victim's first contact with the paddle is with the blade on the side away from the rescuer, he may pull up on this instead of the paddle shaft laid between the kayaks. This happens frequently as the victim wants to surface quickly, and may break the paddle blade.

The Eskimo roll

There are many alternative rolls. The most useful ones in my experience are the screw and the put-across, both using the paddles in the normal paddling grip, but I will first describe the alternative body movements that make up an important part of the roll.

1 The hip flick
This consists of the upward jerk of one hip towards the armpit. Practise this at home. Sit upright on the floor with your legs in front of you as if you were sitting in a kayak. Now lean over to one side and put your elbow on the floor about the length of your forearm from your hip. Roll your legs with your knees together until the side of your knee touches the floor. Now jerk your backside back into the sitting position, keeping your elbow on the floor and dropping your head until your cheek rests close to your shoulder. This is the hip flick that rights your kayak, and it now remains for you to bring your body upright.

The hip flick

Practising the body movement of the hip flick on dry land.

The hip flick

Practising the body movement of the hip flick in a kayak on dry land.

2 The lie-back

When you are upside down in your kayak, lean forwards to one side, so that the flotation in your buoyancy aid will help to bring you close to the surface. As you first pull down on your paddle, start to rotate your body so as to bring your chest to the surface while bringing your hip towards your armpit. The movement of your hip rights the kayak, and you should now be lying on your back on the water with your body out at about right angles to the boat. To complete the movement, continue to pull down on your paddle to bring your body onto the back deck, with the back of your head leaving the water last.

Learning the screw roll

Hold your paddle alongside your kayak with the drive face of the front blade uppermost and the edge nearest your kayak raised slightly. Now push the paddle well forwards while leaning forwards yourself. This is the starting position for the roll, often called the 'wind-up', after which you unwind. Before you capsize, guide the front blade out about 30 cm (1 ft) from the kayak, and the rear blade underneath your hull. You will normally need to do this when you are upside down to ensure that your back paddle blade clears your kayak as you roll. To minimize disorientation, we will start with the paddle sweep from a position where your body is lying on the surface.

Allow yourself to topple over to the side away from your paddle. As your body hits the water, scull your front blade round and use either a hip flick or a lie-back to right your craft. To make best use of the paddle, scull it forwards again when it reaches an angle of about 45° behind

The starting (wind-up) position for the screw roll.

you. This is useful because the closer your blade gets to the kayak, the less leverage you get from it. By bringing the paddle forwards again you will bring it back into the area of maximum leverage, level with your body, so if you fail to get up completely at the first attempt, you will get another chance.

Continue this exercise on both sides until you are able to drop completely upside down before rolling up; you are now only one step away from a complete roll. Finally, capsize towards your paddle, so that you come up on the opposite side.

When you practise, have a companion standing in the water alongside your stern deck, ready to grip your boat and help right it if you need help.

Above *Learning the screw roll with a helper. Topple away from your paddle until your body hits the water. Your helper can support you in this position by holding the rear deck. Scull the paddle round and use a hip flick or lie back to right the kayak.*

Below *A screw roll in detail.*

In rolling a double sea kayak, the front paddler starts the roll first. The stern man joins in when he feels the kayak moving.

The put-across roll

Start in the screw roll wind-up position. Bring your paddle round until it is at right angles to your kayak, with the paddle shaft extending across the hull of your kayak. This is the starting position for the put-across roll. Push the blade up to the surface, leaning well forwards to the surface of the water on the same side. Then pull directly down on the paddle to right yourself.

If you begin the put-across from the screw roll position, you can proceed as for a screw roll by sculling the blade round into the put-across position, gaining extra rolling power before you continue with the put-across. This hybrid roll is often affectionately called a 'screw-across'.

Suggestions for practice

1 Always lean your body towards the surface before you begin your roll. This saves the effort of dragging your body through the water during the roll itself.

2 If your roll is not completely successful, try to retrieve the situation using a recovery stroke.

3 If your rolling starts to get worse rather than better, take a break, and then go back to practising your body movement without your paddles; then ask someone to support your kayak so that you can concentrate on perfecting your paddle movement.

4 It can help a lot to rehearse the roll in your mind whenever you have a quiet moment.

5 As soon as you have mastered the roll, practise in as many different situations as possible. This will make you more adaptable and improve your confidence for the time when you capsize accidentally.

Rolling in surf

Use the power in the waves to help you roll up. Broadside on, you will find it easier to roll up into an oncoming wave than to roll up on the side away from it.

Start in small broken waves, making sure that the water is deep enough. Turn broadside to the oncoming wave and capsize, setting your paddles up for a roll into the wave. Wait until you feel the thrust of the wave hitting your paddle and kayak before rolling up gently. The force of the wave pushing your boat along the surface will do most of the work if your timing is reasonable, leaving you bracing on the wave.

Rolling in strong winds

If you capsize in strong winds, your kayak will be blown sideways across the water with your body trailing behind, in much the same way as in surf. Roll up into the wind to take advantage of this.

Rolling in a tidal race

This is similar to rolling in a rapid river. If you are broadside to the stream your body will be carried towards the surface on the downstream side, so it is much easier to roll up on this side. As waves break against the stream, you will also be rolling up into the oncoming waves, as in surf and on white water rivers.

If you are rolling in the aerated water behind a large breaker, use the *storm roll*. Instead of making the wide surface sweep of the screw roll, take your paddle deep alongside your kayak where the blade can grip the less aerated water beneath the surface. (See Chapter 12, tidal races and overfalls.)

The paddle brace is an essential skill for sea kayaking. It is adapted for a wide variety of uses.

The low brace

Present the back of the paddle blade to the water to one side of the kayak. With your elbow bent, push downwards onto the paddle to maintain your balance. Your elbow should be above the paddle shaft. Keep the shaft as low to the water as possible, whether it lies across the deck or alongside your kayak.

The high brace

Present the drive face of the paddle to the water. With your elbow bent beneath the shaft, pull downwards to balance yourself. Keep the shaft as horizontal as possible. The action is similar to hanging from a bar doing chin-ups.

A low brace (right), with the elbows above the paddle shaft, is used (below) to turn the kayak on the crest of a wave.

Bracing into breaking waves

Use the paddle brace to keep your balance when you're hit from the side by a breaking wave. If the waves are small, use the low brace. Place the paddle on top of the wave and tilt the kayak towards the break. The kayak will be pushed sideways, while the paddle planes across the surface maintaining support. Push down on the paddle to bring the kayak upright.

On larger waves, use the high brace. Place the blade high on the wave. Keep the other blade

A high brace (above), with elbows below the paddle shaft, is used for support (top) on a large wave while the kayak is carried sideways towards the shore.

as low as possible. The paddle should slope upwards towards the crest of the wave. Alternatively, keep the paddle horizontal. When the kayak is carried sideways the blade will plane across the water providing support rather than digging in. Keep your elbow bent throughout this manoeuvre: if your arm is fully extended and your blade is steeply angled, the force of the wave is capable of dislocating your shoulder. Pull down on the paddle to bring your body upright, although the kayak should remain tilted towards the break.

Forward movement can still be maintained if you are caught by a breaking crest, by moving the paddle brace towards the stern of the kayak. This will slow the stern slightly, allowing the

bow to drop, and the kayak will move along the wave at the same time as travelling sideways. Considerable acceleration can be gained in this way and the extra momentum will carry you for quite some distance after the crest has gone.

When paddling out through steep waves, especially in surf or tidal races, you can use a low brace to maintain balance as the bow lifts up through a crest and drops into the following trough.

In a following sea, a low brace will provide stability and confidence if you trail the blade a couple of feet out to one side. Because the blade is flat on the water and under very little pressure, steering is not affected. This technique is particularly useful when inexperienced paddlers are paddling in a steep following sea, when they might be nervous of surfing forwards.

The low paddle brace is useful in steep launches as described in Chapter 4. You can also use it to steady the kayak when you want to look behind you. For best effect, increase your speed slightly and raise your blade a little at its leading edge. However, if you are paddling into strong headwinds, then the wind will rapidly push you backwards making the blade dive if you are not wary. A better procedure under these circumstances is to apply a forward power stroke on one side while looking over the opposite shoulder. This not only gives more stability under the circumstances, but also prevents you being blown backwards.

9 Forward paddling technique

It is best to paddle a sea kayak with the blades passing down close alongside the boat. Try to maintain a good trunk rotation, originating with pressure on the footrest on the same side as each paddle stroke. Forward paddling is what you spend most time doing, so it is worth developing a really efficient style.

A following sea

Although perhaps a little daunting for many beginners, paddling with a following sea can give you an exhilarating and rapid ride. The skill is knowing when to paddle, when to stop paddling, steer and let the wave do the work, and when to pause to wait for the next wave. Start with fairly small wind-blown waves. Paddle forwards downwind and you will find that the bow of your kayak will rise and fall as waves overtake you. Wait until your bow has reached its highest point and begins to drop, and then make two or three vigorous paddle strokes while leaning your weight forwards. Your kayak should surge forward on the face of the wave that is raising your stern. Pause, and steer with a stern rudder if necessary. As soon as the kayak stalls, and the bow rises once more, wait and prepare yourself for another

Below *A following sea*

couple of paddle strokes. Your paddling will take up a different rhythm to match the waves, with a short burst of activity followed by a pause. You may feel as though, by your periods of steering and inactivity, you are not progressing as rapidly as you would if you were keeping up a steady paddling pace. This is an illusion. You travel faster by using the waves.

When you have bigger waves behind you, particularly a heavy swell, the waves travel faster and you will need more speed in order to catch them. Long fast sea kayaks can make use of waves that short slow ones cannot catch. However, there comes a point at which the waves are really too fast for you to be able to gain much advantage. To read a following sea, look ahead at the wave that has just passed you rather than at the one following. The steeper the wall of water ahead of you, the steeper the following wave, because they share the same trough.

Short paddles with broad blades give better acceleration for catching waves than long narrow ones.

The stern rudder

Use your stern rudder for steering downwind or while running down a wave. The rudder is normally applied at the end of a forward paddle stroke. Make your normal forward paddle stroke till the blade is level with your hip. With the edge onto the water, slice the blade out diagonally backwards, then bring it back to the stern in a stern sweep. The blade is then angled with the upper edge of the blade tilted towards the kayak, and is held in position until the desired correction is achieved. The kayak will turn to the right if the paddle is held on the left.

The alternative use of a stern rudder is to apply the blade to the opposite side of the kayak but with the upper edge of the blade angled away from the boat. The kayak will turn to the right if the paddle is held on the right.

If you are travelling diagonally downwind, most kayaks will show a tendency to broach. A stern rudder on the side of the approaching waves, angled with the upper edge towards the kayak will make balancing easier in a strong wind than a stern rudder on the downwind side, when the kayak will tend to be blown sideways over the paddle.

Paddling forwards in strong winds

You shouldn't need to change your paddling style. Long paddles, however, are more likely to be caught by the wind than short ones, so some paddlers advocate lowering the paddles into a series of sweep strokes when the wind is strong. However, this lowers the efficiency of the paddle stroke just when you need maximum power. I have paddled in winds of over 70 knots with fairly short paddles without the need to modify my technique.

The stern rudder. With the upper edge of the blade tilted away from the kayak, the kayak turns towards the paddle (left in this case).

With the blade upright in the neutral position, the kayak runs straight.

With the upper edge of the blade tilted towards the kayak, the kayak turns to the right, away from the paddle.

Tides are caused by the gravitational pull of the moon and the sun. The rise and fall of the level of the sea is accompanied by a movement to and fro of the sea water, known as tidal streams. Tidal streams can be of enormous help to a sea paddler, provided that the journey is well planned. The level of the tide is important for launching and landing. A look at a set of tide tables will show the time and the height of high and low tide, for a given place, here Greenport.

GREENPORT TIDES

| | HIGH WATER | | | | | | LOW WATER | | | | | | SUN | |
| | Morning | | | Afternoon | | | Morning | | | Afternoon | | | Rise | Set |
Date	Time	Ht. mts.	Ht. feet	Time	Ht. mts.	Ht. feet	Time	Ht. mts.	Ht. feet	Time	Ht. mts.	Ht. feet	a.m.	p.m.
1 Sun	05 04	7.2	23.6	17 25	7.3	24.1	11 25	3.4	11.1				08 27	16 03
2 Mon	06 08	7.1	23.4	18 32	7.3	23.8	00 18	3.1	10.3	12 38	3.4	11.3	08 27	16 05
3 Tue	07 16	7.3	23.9	19 41	7.4	24.3	01 27	3.1	10.1	13 49	3.2	10.7	08 27	16 06
4 Wed	08 16	7.6	25.0	20 42	7.7	25.3	02 30	2.9	9.4	14 54	2.9	9.5	08 27	16 07
5 Thu	09 10	8.1	26.5	21 34	8.1	26.6	03 27	2.5	8.3	15 49	2.5	8.1	08 26	16 08
6 Fri	09 56	8.5	27.9	22 20	8.5	27.9	04 16	2.2	7.1	16 41	2.0	6.6	08 26	16 10
7 Sat	10 41	8.9	29.2	23 05	8.8	29.0	05 02	1.8	6.0	17 29	1.6	5.3	08 25	16 11
8 Sun	11 25	9.2	30.3				05 47	1.5	5.0	18 17	1.2	4.1	08 25	16 12
9 Mon				12 10	9.5	31.1	06 32	1.3	4.2	19 03	1.0	3.2	08 24	16 14
10 Tue	00 34	9.2	30.3	12 53	9.6	31.5	07 16	1.2	3.8	19 47	0.8	2.7	08 24	16 15
11 Wed	01 19	9.2	30.3	13 38	9.6	31.5	07 58	1.2	3.8	20 30	0.8	2.7	08 23	16 17
12 Thu	02 04	9.1	29.8	14 23	9.5	31.1	08 40	1.3	4.3	21 14	1.0	3.4	08 22	16 18
13 Fri	02 50	8.8	28.9	15 10	9.2	30.2	09 24	1.6	5.2	21 58	1.4	4.5	08 21	16 20
14 Sat	03 38	8.5	27.8	16 00	8.8	28.9	10 12	1.9	6.4	22 48	1.8	5.9	08 20	16 22
15 Sun	04 33	8.1	26.5	16 59	8.4	27.4	11 08	2.3	7.7	23 47	2.2	7.4	08 19	16 23
16 Mon	05 39	7.7	25.4	18 10	8.0	26.2				12 17	2.6	8.7	08 18	16 25
17 Tue	06 56	7.6	24.9	19 28	7.8	25.6	00 59	2.6	8.4	13 40	2.7	8.9	08 17	16 27
18 Wed	08 11	7.8	25.5	20 42	7.9	26.1	02 18	2.6	8.6	14 58	2.5	8.2	08 16	16 28
19 Thu	09 17	8.1	26.7	21 45	8.2	27.0	03 28	2.4	8.0	16 07	2.1	7.0	08 15	16 30
20 Fri	10 10	8.5	28.0	22 35	8.5	28.0	04 26	2.1	7.0	17 02	1.7	5.7	08 14	16 32
21 Sat	10 57	8.9	29.0	23 19	8.7	28.7	05 15	1.9	6.2	17 50	1.5	4.8	08 13	16 34
22 Sun	11 36	9.1	29.7				05 56	1.7	5.6	18 29	1.3	4.3	08 12	16 36
23 Mon				12 12	9.1	30.0	06 31	1.6	5.2	19 06	1.3	4.2	08 10	16 37
24 Tue	00 32	8.9	29.1	12 46	9.1	29.9	07 03	1.6	5.1	19 37	1.4	4.4	08 09	16 39
25 Wed	01 04	8.8	28.9	13 19	9.0	29.6	07 33	1.6	5.3	20 06	1.5	4.8	08 08	16 41
26 Thu	01 35	8.7	28.4	13 49	8.8	29.0	08 06	1.8	5.8	20 33	1.7	5.5	08 06	16 43
27 Fri	02 08	8.5	27.8	14 20	8.6	28.2	08 30	2.0	6.5	21 01	2.0	6.4	08 05	16 45
28 Sat	02 40	8.2	26.9	14 53	8.3	27.1	09 03	2.3	7.5	21 34	2.3	7.6	08 03	16 47
29 Sun	03 14	7.9	25.8	15 28	7.9	25.9	09 38	2.7	8.7	22 10	2.7	9.0	08 02	16 49
30 Mon	03 56	7.5	24.6	16 14	7.5	24.5	10 23	3.1	10.1	23 01	3.2	10.4	08 00	16 51
31 Tue	04 52	7.1	23.5	17 19	7.1	23.2	11 25	3.4	11.2				07 58	16 53

ADD ONE HOUR FROM 0100 MARCH 26th TO 0100 OCTOBER 29th

Let's look at the morning of January 1st. High water will be at 0504 hours at Greenport. At this time the height of the water will be 7.2 m or 23.6 ft. This is a height relative to *chart datum* for Greenport, which is approximately the shallowest the water can ever be expected to get, weather conditions excepted (see Chapter 13, air pressure and tides). Looking at the height of the tide at low water, 3.4 m (11.1 ft), we can calculate that the *range* of the tide at Greenport will be 7.2–3.4 m or 3.8 m (12.5 ft).

If we compare this figure with the *range* of the tide on the morning of January 22nd, which is 9.1 m minus 1.7 m (29.7 ft minus 5.6 ft) which equals 7.4 m (24.1 ft), we can see there is quite a considerable variation in the range of the tide. But why should this be?

Spring and neap tides

The answer is that the gravity of the sun sometimes combines with that of the moon to create a big tide, and is at other times out of alignment with the gravity of the moon creating a smaller range. When the sun and moon are in line with the earth, we view the moon as either full or new. In the case of the full moon, the sun is lighting the whole of the face visible from earth, and in the case of a new moon, the sun is lighting only that face of the moon invisible from earth, leaving us in view of the dark side. In both cases we have a strong combined pull on the earth making the tides greater than average. We call them *spring tides* (nothing to do with the season of the year!).

When the sun and moon create a right angle with the earth, the moon is viewed as a half moon, and the tidal range is at its least. This is known as a *neap tide*. If we look again at the January tide tables, we see that there will be a spring tide on the 10th/11th and again on the 23rd, and a neap tide on the 2nd and 16th. In other words spring tides occur about once a fortnight, and twice in a lunar month, alternating with neaps.

If we look up the dates of the full and new moon for the same month, we find that the new moon occurs on the 7th and the full moon on the 20th. In other words, the greatest tidal ranges are experienced two or three days *after* the full or new moon. This is a useful fact to remember, so that you can get some idea of how the tides are going to affect you by observing the moon. Unfortunately the pattern is not quite as straightforward as this. The position of the moon relative to the earth varies throughout the year creating bigger spring tides at some times of the year than at others. This can be seen when you look through the tide tables for a year. The greatest tidal range observed for Greenport will be 10.3 m (33.8 ft) as compared with 7.4 m (24.1 ft) on January 22nd. Both are spring tides.

Working with the tides

Now, how does this affect you as a sea kayaker? Well, it does so in two major ways. Firstly, all the water that comes and goes as the tide rises and falls actually travels along the coast as a

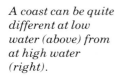

A coast can be quite different at low water (above) from at high water (right).

tidal stream. When there is a spring tide, more water moves in the same time, so the tidal streams are greater. In places in the Faeroe Islands, such tidal streams attain rates of 12 knots, which compares badly with the 6 knots an experienced paddler might expect to achieve even in calm water.

The second way the tide will affect you is by the amount of foreshore that becomes exposed at low tide, and by how far the tide reaches at high tide. For example, the foreshore stretches out for over two miles of rock and sand to the south-east of La Rocque in Jersey, while the water rises to within feet of the road at high water on the same day, on a big spring tide. Imagine trying to carry your kayak to your car at low tide! On a similar low tide one could land and stroll around on the beach on Lundy Island,

whereas at high tide there is no beach beneath the cliffs.

Tidal stream atlases are available for some coastal areas, displaying the direction of the tide hour by hour throughout the tidal cycle by means of arrows. The boldness of the print used for the arrows indicates the strength of the stream. The approximate rate of the tide at mean neaps and mean spring tides is given in places as numbers. For example, an arrow with the figures 06,17 printed alongside indicates a mean neap rate of 0.6 knots and a mean spring rate of 1.7 knots. Thus if we know from the tide tables whether we are experiencing neaps or springs, or in between, and we know what time high water will be, then we can tell from the tidal stream charts what rate of tide in what direction to expect at any one place at any time during the day. This is a very useful basis for planning a coastal journey with the tide.

Similar information is displayed on admiralty charts but in tabular form, referring to points on the chart identified by a diamond-shaped lozenge around a letter, e.g. ⟨F⟩. The information given looks like this:

		Rate (Kn)	
	53° 10.0' N 4° 6.2' W		
Hours	Dir	Sp	Np
Before HW 6	050	0.8	0.4
5	050	3.2	1.6
4	047	4.1	2.0
3	043	4.2	2.0
2	041	3.1	1.5
1	040	2.8	1.4
HW	220	2.0	1.0
After HW 1	222	1.0	0.5
2	218	3.3	1.6
3	216	4.1	2.1
4	217	4.2	2.1
5	218	3.3	1.6
6	055	2.8	1.4

Directions are given from true north so a 90° stream flows towards the east. So for example, at high water the stream is heading towards 220° true at about 2 knots at springs. To calculate the compass direction of the stream, you will need to correct for magnetic variation.

It is convenient to assume that the direction and rate for any tabulated time remain constant for the half hour before and after that time also. Referring to the table, at 4 hours before HW we see a direction of 47° at a spring rate of 4.1 knots. We assume that this is the case for the whole period between 4½ hours before and 3½ hours before HW.

The tidal stream information will refer to the HW at a given place; not necessarily the place to which your own tide tables refer. However, *tidal constants,* or *tidal differences,* are commonly given with tide tables enabling you to add or subtract given values from the times at one port to give you those for places of secondary import- ance in the wider area.

Another method of displaying tidal streams on an admiralty chart is by means of isolated arrows, which indicate the direction of the stream, and which may or may not have accom- panying tidal rates. An arrow with flight feathers indicates the direction of the *flood tide* (rising tide). An arrow without flight feathers indicates the direction of the *ebb tide* (falling tide). Rates for spring or neap tides given here are normally mean rates, and the flight feathers bear no rela- tionship to the speed of the tide, unlike the arrows in some weather maps.

Sp1.5 Np 0.7 (Direction of flood tide)
(Direction of ebb tide)

Tidal information is also given in nautical almanacs and Admiralty Pilots. Local yachting and kayaking guides often give important details such as the times of changes in the direction of streams, the behaviour of eddies that may form, and the positions of rough water caused by the tide, particularly in areas where the charts do not show sufficient detail.

The rule of twelfths

The hourly rate of rise or fall of the tide through the tidal cycle can be predicted roughly using the twelfths rule. This states that during the first hour following low water, the tide will rise by one twelfth of the total range expected. In the second hour it will rise by a further two twelfths, in the third and fourth hour by three twelfths in each, in the fifth hour by another two twelfths and in the last hour up to high water by the remaining one twelfth of the range. This means that the tide is rising most rapidly during the two middle hours of the tidal rise. The fall of the tide is governed by the same rule. Although you might deduce that the behaviour of tide streams will also follow the same rule, flowing at their fastest during the middle two hours of rise or fall, unfortunately this is not always the case. In some places the slack period falls at this time and the tide streams are at their maximum at high or low water. Always check your tidal stream information!

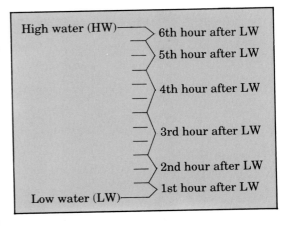

The twelfths rule

11 Understanding charts

Charts give a wealth of useful information to the sea kayaker that is normally totally absent from topographical maps. Do use them.

When you pick up an unfamiliar chart, look first for the title positioned in an area of the chart of little navigational importance. This is followed by an amount of useful information. Here will be a statement as to whether depths are in metres or fathoms. (A fathom is 6 ft.) Charts show depths of water measured below chart datum (chart datum usually represents the level of the lowest astronomical tide) and the height of the foreshore measured above chart datum. All heights on land above the foreshore are normally measured from the level of mean high water, springs. The projection of the chart and sources of data are given together with other information and relevant warnings. Always check through these data first when you pick up an unfamiliar chart.

Next, find a scale. Most sea paddlers work in nautical miles. A nautical mile (usually simply referred to as a mile when talking about the sea) is equal to one sixtieth of a degree, or one minute, of latitude. Latitude is graduated down the sides of the chart, and you should measure distances on the chart from the scale at the same latitude as the section you are measuring. This is because the method of projecting charts to get a curved section of the globe onto flat paper, often leads to the scale at one end of the chart differing from the scale at the other end. Never mistake the degree of longitude at the top and bottom of the chart with latitude. Lines of longitude converge to the poles and do not indicate nautical miles. *Always measure from the side of the chart.*

On British metric charts, land is shown in yellow, all land that is covered at high tide and uncovered at low tide during the greatest astronomical tides is coloured green, and the sea is white, with the 10 m depth contour edged in blue and all water of less than 5 m coloured blue. All other information is given in either magenta or black. There are myriad symbols used on the chart, so a booklet is published by the Admiralty as a key, sold as chart number 5011. These are some of the most important symbols.

2_5 means water to a depth of 2.5 m below chart datum.

3_7 means the land here dries to a height of 3.7 m above chart datum. This is a *drying height.*

≈ means a tide race or overfall. (See Chapter 12.)

⚹ (asterisk in black, flash in magenta) indicates a light.

⁜ indicates an underwater rock with 2 m (6.6 ft) or less water over it at chart datum.

⁜ indicates a rock awash at chart datum.

Waves

Sea waves are of three kinds: wind blown waves produced by the wind that is blowing there and then; swell that is produced by winds elsewhere; and waves caused by the flow of water, such as tidal streams and ocean currents.

Let's look at the formation of waves in deep water first. The type of waves we normally encounter are *gravitational waves*. These will continue to travel through the water even when the wind has dropped away, but they do not travel as fast as the wind that creates them. However, they frequently outstrip the weather systems around which the winds blow and can arrive at the beach long before the weather system arrives, giving warning of its approach. By contrast, *capillary waves* are the wavelets that tear across the surface heralding gusts of wind. These travel at the same speed as the wind that creates them, warning us to be ready when a gust hits. They die away immediately the wind dies.

The size of gravitational waves depends on several factors.

1 The wind strength. The stronger the wind, the more energy is available to build up waves. We actually estimate the strength of the wind according to the state of the sea.

2 The fetch. This is the distance over which the wind may blow. Gale force winds never produce large waves on a small pond, but they do in the open ocean.

3 The duration of the wind. It takes time for a steady wind to produce its maximum wave size. A gale force wind may take 2 days to build waves up to their maximum for the wind strength.

4 The size of the waves will be diminished if they meet waves from an opposing direction, if they meet an opposing tidal stream or current, or if there is heavy rain or snow. They will also be flattened by subsequent winds in opposing directions.

Wind-blown waves, created by the wind blowing there and then, tend to be irregular, sharp-crested and chaotic, particularly when the wind is in the process of changing direction, as it does with the progress of weather systems around which winds circulate. Waves run out in all directions from weather systems, sometimes merging and reinforcing each other and sometimes opposing and flattening each other. Sea-farers call this rather chaotic spawning ground for waves a 'sea'. However, at a distance from this 'wave generator', the waves begin to sort themselves out into a more even wavelength, and the wave form becomes more rounded at the crest. This type of wave is called a *swell*. Swells can travel thousands of miles. As they travel, their wavelength (the distance from crest to crest) and speed increase. Young swells are steeper, slower and closer together than more mature swells. Old swells attain speeds of over 50 knots, and have been observed with a period (the time taken for successive crests to pass a given point) of as much as 30 seconds.

Because waves travel at different speeds, those travelling faster will catch up with and overtake slower ones. When one wave catches up with another, the resulting wave will be larger than before. When the waves are out of phase and one crest coincides with the trough of another wave pattern, then the two cancel each other out to flatten the water. Thus we experience a series of larger waves, called a *set*, followed by a *lull*, where we see much smaller or even no waves. Very old swells will have much longer lulls between sets than younger swells, which means easier launching and landing if you time it right.

Sometimes swell approaches from two very different directions. For convenience let's say the waves approach each other at right angles. Wherever a crest crosses a trough the wave will be flattened, and wherever a crest crosses a crest, the wave height will increase. Wherever a trough meets another trough we find an extra deep hole. The resulting sea will consist of criss-crossing mounds rather than simple walls of water; quite a different visual effect and quite a different surface on which to paddle.

Breaking waves

1 Waves in shallow water

Swells start to alter in shape when the depth of the water becomes less than half the wavelength. For example, a swell with a wavelength of 90 m (300 ft) will start to 'feel bottom' when the depth is less than 45 m (150 ft). Once waves feel bottom, they begin to slow down, become closer together and steepen. If the wavelength is fifty times or more greater than the wave height in deep water, then the wave will also increase in height when

Clapotis occurs when an incoming wave meets a rebounding wave. The resulting unstable mass of water explodes in all directions.

it reaches shallower water. The wave will steepen until the water is about 1.3 times the height of the wave at that time, then it will break. Onshore winds will cause waves to break in deeper water, maybe even at a point where the depth is twice the wave height. With an offshore breeze, old swells with a long wave-length may be held up until the depth of water is less than three quarters of the height of the wave.

The way in which a wave breaks is determined by the shape of the sea bed. If the sea bed shelves gently, then the wave will gradually steepen and then break at some distance from the shore, as seen on a surf beach. If the shore shelves steeply, then the wave will steepen abruptly and collapse immediately, breaking with explosive force onto the beach itself. Such waves are called *dumpers*, and can be very dangerous. Dumpers can produce strong undertows – currents running out to sea along the sea bed.

Isolated rocks that are covered with water are normally marked on the chart. In swell conditions it is important to note their position as you paddle because the depth of water covering them may well permit all but the largest swells to pass over unbroken, just occasionally breaking with great power when a particularly large swell arrives. In America they call such waves *boomers*. I have been caught out by boomers off South-West Cornwall, and in Iceland. Both sit-

Waves created by moving water

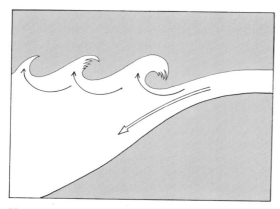

Haystacks *formed in an overfall where fast-flowing constricted water meets deeper water. Haystacks are also formed in races downstream of a constriction.*

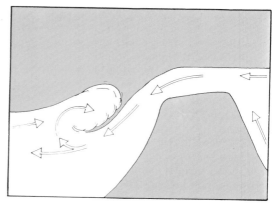

A **stopper wave** *produced in an overfall at the base of a steep drop.*

uations were dramatic enough for the memory to remain clear after many years. Be cautious! Learn the symbols for rocks that cover and uncover, that are awash at chart datum, and are covered by 2 m (6.6 ft) or less of water at chart datum. These are the rocks most likely to cause boomers, depending on the depth of water covering them and the state of the tide. (See Chapter 11.)

Waves rebound from cliffs and very steep shores and collide with oncoming waves. Although the depth of water may be able to support each wave individually, it cannot support the increased height formed when two steep waves combine. The result is a suddenly unstable mass of water which explodes in all directions. This is called *clapotis*.

2 Waves breaking as a result of the wind
In open water, the wind speed will determine the nature and frequency of breaking waves. We estimate wind strength by observing the state of such a sea. (See Chapter 13 for the Beaufort wind scale.)

3 Waves created by moving water
When a tidal stream accelerates due to a constriction in the width of a channel, then waves are formed. These waves are usually pointed standing waves, often with breaking crests, resembling the 'haystacks' that are found on white-water rivers. True standing waves remain in the same position relative to the rapid, but on the sea, the presence of swell and wind-blown waves complicates the pattern, and so we find waves which move up against the stream. Such an area of constriction, together with its associated rough water, is known as a *tidal race*. The fast-flowing water acts in a similar way to a beach, slowing the base of the wave as though it were feeling bottom, steepening the face, often to the point of breaking, and bringing crests closer together.

An *overfall* occurs where a tidal stream is forced up and over a ledge or shoal at speed. The acceleration of the water results in waves similar to those of a tidal race. However, if water builds up behind a ledge to form a steep drop, then a vertically circulating eddy is formed. This is called a *stopper* wave because of the effect it has on a paddler trying to pass through it. Interference from swell causes this constantly-breaking wave to surge, so that the height of the fall of water, and with it the holding power of the stopper, fluctuates.

Below *Refraction round a small island (left) causes clapotis behind it.*

Wave refraction

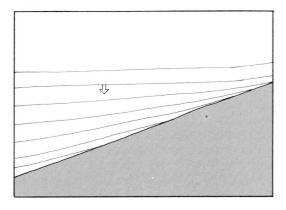

Wave refraction.

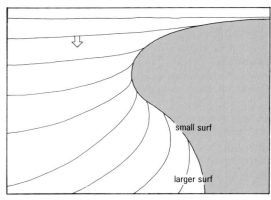

small surf

larger surf

Wave refraction around a headland.

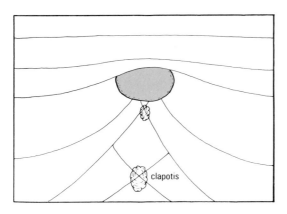

clapotis

Refraction around a small island to cause clapotis behind it.

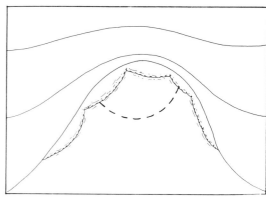

A horseshoe break over a shoal, caused by refraction.

Wave refraction

When waves approach a coastline at an angle, then one end of the swell will feel bottom first and slow down, causing the wave to bend round towards the shore. This is known as *refraction*. Refraction can cause waves to bend around headlands over 180 degrees or more, to reach beaches that might otherwise be sheltered. Refraction can also cause waves to bend around shoals or small islands to meet almost head-on at the 'sheltered' side, often causing clapotis. It is refraction that is responsible for the horseshoe shape of waves breaking over isolated rocks.

Refraction of waves on a surf beach may give rise to areas of *convergence*, where waves will be compressed, increasing the size of the wave, and

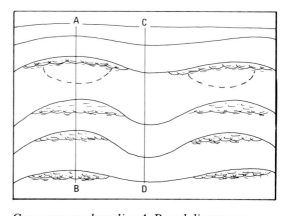

A   C

B   D

Convergence along line A-B and divergence along line C-D. Divergence in this case gives a sheltered route out to sea.

areas of *divergence*, which can cause passages from the shore where there is no significant wave break at all. Such major zones of divergence make for ideal launching and landing places through surf, but are normally found only where there are sandbanks offshore.

Tidal races and overfalls

The characteristics of tidal streams resemble those of water flowing in a river. Where the stream is constricted in depth or width, it will increase in speed. A tidal race is caused by water squeezed around a headland, or between two shores. It is called an overfall if there is a constriction in the depth.

Both overfalls and races are potentially hazardous places requiring care, especially if there is any swell or wind. The sea is at its most violent when the wind blows against the tide. The sea is much rougher than you would expect for that wind speed. Even a light breeze against a race or overfall is sufficient to produce a rough sea. Even though a wind blowing with the tide tends to quieten a sea, it is still likely to be rougher here than elsewhere. Waves break against the tide so if you paddle with the tide you will meet the breaking waves head on.

When you plan a journey to pass through such areas, take careful note of the wind direction relative to the exact direction of the stream in the race or overfall, which may differ from that of the general lie of the coast. Rescues in races and overfalls can be difficult, so be sure of the ability of the group and, if in doubt, wait until the tide has slackened, or avoid the worst of the rough water by hugging the shore or passing well out to sea where the stream may be much weaker. Study the local pilot and gain local knowledge if possible.

Below *At the up-tide end of a tidal race.*

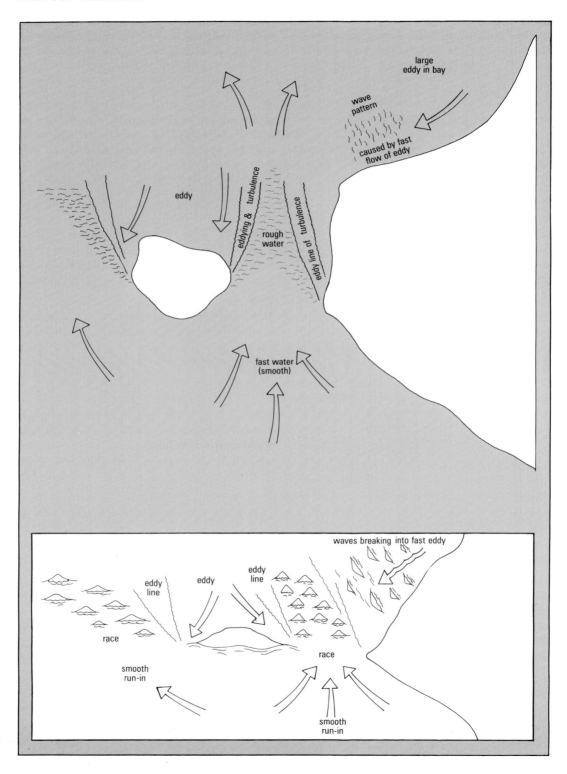

Tidal races

Tidal races can offer a lot of good fun to the competent paddler. Typically, a smooth run-in of fast water where the stream is constricted erupts into a series of standing waves on the downtide end of the constriction. These standing waves normally move slowly upstream, disappearing to leave the smooth run-in unaffected. The upstream waves are usually the largest, followed by smaller and smaller waves as you get further from the constriction. In a large tidal race the effect may be felt at a distance of several miles downtide. The first waves are usually the best for surfing on, so catch a wave before you are swept too far downstream, otherwise a return to the 'front' becomes difficult or impossible. Watch the waves in front of you while you surf. The criss-crossing wave patterns rarely give you a perfectly clean wave, so aim for the deepest 'hole' you can see at any time, rather than looking over your shoulder at what is behind. Although a wave may appear to be very big and steep, and it may look as if just a couple of paddle strokes would be required to catch a ride, in fact, because of the speed of the tide running through the waves, it demands more effort. However, once on a wave, you should get a long ride, slowly making your way to the front of the race to emerge with smooth water ahead of you.

Surfing is normally best when the tide is not at its fastest. When a very fast tide is encountered, waves become difficult to catch unless they are breaking or almost breaking. However, if an exhilarating run downtide through a race is what you're after, then there is little to beat a maximum rate descent.

Overfalls

Overfalls have the characteristics of tidal races, plus a few additional features. Water rushing over rocks and ledges can produce vertical eddies or stoppers, with a tow-back (water returning from downstream back along the surface to the stopper). Where rocks are exposed, the chutes of water that rush between them cause powerful eddies, with surges and boils. The eddy lines

A typical tidal situation at a headland, complicated by the presence of a small offshore island.

create an impressively turbulent no-man's-land between each eddy and stream. It is the presence of eddies behind exposed rocks that make overfalls such good playgrounds and training grounds. After an energetic burst of surfing, a quick retreat into an eddy will enable you to return to the top of the rapid and to rest. However, because larger sets of waves can expose rocks that have previously been covered, it is safer to play in overfalls on a rising tide when the positions of rocks can be noted early on.

Be careful when you cross from an eddy into the main stream. Tilt the kayak away from the oncoming water to prevent it from piling up on your deck and capsizing you. There are three suitable approaches.

Approach from the eddy in an upstream direction and allow the current to turn your kayak downstream as you cross the eddy line. This is best performed from an angle of about 45 degrees to the current, using a low brace on the downstream side for support. Approach the eddy line with a little speed and, as the bow crosses the eddy line and you feel the kayak begin to turn, tilt into the turn and perform a low brace. The fast-moving water will do all the work in turning the boat; you need to maintain your balance and to paddle out into the stream before your kayak has turned completely downstream. If you allow the kayak to turn completely, it will tend to get caught on the eddy line.

Alternatively, approach the eddy line in an upstream direction as before, but maintain the same angle of attack until you are well out into the main stream. This will put you in a good position for catching waves. You should still tilt the kayak away from the current, but the angle of approach to the eddy line needs to be less than 45 degrees; very little angle at all is required. As the bow crosses the eddy line, tilt the kayak from the current and perform a forward sweep stroke on the downstream side before you start to paddle forward again. If you cross the eddy line quickly, not giving the current time to turn the kayak, you should end up positioned for a ferry-glide across the current.

The third approach is to paddle diagonally across the eddy line in a downstream direction. With this method, you don't have to tilt the kayak. The eddy line becomes increasingly broad downstream of the obstacle producing it, so the kayak may spin round, or at least weave a path along the eddy line instead of crossing it.

Turning on an eddy line. Approach the eddy in an upstream direction. Let the current turn your kayak downstream. As the bow crosses the eddy line and you feel the kayak begin to turn, tilt into the turn and perform a low brace. Paddle out into the stream before your kayak turns completely downstream.

Eddy lines can be quite narrow and well defined close behind an obstacle, but there can be quite a difference in water level between the eddy and the water rushing past, so that you have to 'climb out' of the eddy. Further downtide the eddy line becomes broader, frequently wider than the length of a sea kayak, and filled with boils and small whirlpools. Still further downtide the eddy line loses its violence as the eddy loses its strength.

Safety

Tidal races and overfalls can cause problems. It is not always easy to predict what the conditions will be like when the sea elsewhere seems quite placid. Try to look for indicators such as the gentle ground swell that lifts you gently and almost imperceptibly up and down, and which can cause very heavy water in tidal races and overfalls. Swell is often most apparent near rocks

Crossing an eddy line. Approach the eddy line in an upstream direction. Keep the same angle of attack until you are well out into the main stream. As the bow crosses the eddy line, tilt the kayak from the current and perform a forward sweep stroke on the downstream side before you start to paddle forward again.

and cliffs, where the white breaking water sprays up to surprising heights. When you get closer to the race, establish a plan of action, and assess the severity of your chosen route. If in doubt, retreat to safer water before you are committed. The calm water leading into a race can flow swiftly! Agree on hand signals to be used. In event of a capsize, the victim will be much more visible if he holds his paddle vertically above his head. Otherwise it can be difficult to spot a cap-

sized kayak with swimmer, even at quite close range. Paddling close together to use shouted or whistled signals is not often practical or safe if conditions are rough. Deep-water rescues can also be difficult and dangerous. You may need to use a long tow-line to tow a victim into calmer water for a rescue, or wait until he has been flushed through the worst of the broken water.

A group can rapidly become spread out when moving from an eddy into fast water. A paddler

Above *In the event of a capsize, a paddle held vertically is much more visible than a kayak and swimmer, even at quite close range.*

in a tide race may easily cover 100 m in just 15 seconds, while the next paddler is simply preparing to cross the eddy line. Paddlers wishing to keep together should cross the eddy line either at the same time or in very quick succession, and at an acute angle to the current so as to ferry glide out. The group can then turn together to paddle downstream.

You can build up your confidence in tidal races by first paddling a few circuits, joining the fast water from the top of an eddy, paddling down through the waves and regaining the eddy further downstream. This is the most straightforward exercise. Next, instead of paddling downstream, allow the tide to do the work, paddling only when absolutely necessary. Then allow yourself to drift sideways through the race, bracing on broken waves when necessary, or paddling forwards or backwards to avoid breaking crests. Finally, drift through backwards, perhaps catching a few rides on the way.

Small headlands often produce suitable races on spring tides, yet are not always marked as overfalls or races on the chart. Such areas can make good training grounds, where the water is not too fast. Look for clearly-defined eddies where you can rest and regroup, and try to establish a set of transit marks on shore or some other back marker to help keep the group together.

Finally, bear in mind that the ferocity of a race will depend on:

1 The wind strength, and its direction.

2 The swell.

3 The strength of the tide; not only springs or neaps, but also which part of the flood or ebb you are at. Gain local knowledge about each particular race or overfall. For example, Penrhyn Mawr overfall on Anglesey only works on the flood tide, as on the ebb it is sheltered from the force of the tide by headlands to the north. The Bitches overfall in Ramsey Sound, Pembrokeshire moves at about its fastest at high water. Paddlers occasionally get a rude awakening here, having assumed that they would find slack water at high tide!

4 The height of the tide. Some overfalls produce the best conditions at certain water levels, and they may experience these water levels for longer on a neap tide than on a spring.

Before setting out onto the sea, check the weather forecast. To interpret a forecast you will need to understand a certain amount about the weather. In time you should be able to develop quite an eye for conditions, but you will need some pointers and some practice.

Wind

Wind is one of the most important aspects of weather for the sea kayaker. Wind is referred to by its direction of origin: a south wind comes from the south. The wind speed is usually expressed as a number on the Beaufort scale, or as a speed in knots.

The wind speed is determined by the pressure gradient; the greater the pressure gradient, the stronger the wind. Pressure gradient is the difference in air pressure over a given distance. If there is a difference of, say 8 millibars over 50 miles, the wind will not be as strong as if the difference were 12 millibars.

If the wind changes direction clockwise, for example from south to south-west, it is said to

The Beaufort wind scale

Force	Speed (knots)	Description	Sea conditions	Sea state
0	1 or less	Calm	Like a mirror.	Smooth
1	1–3	Light air	Ripples like scales.	Calm
2	4–6	Light breeze	Small wavelets, glassy crests, not breaking.	Calm
3	7–10	Gentle breeze	Large wavelets, crests begin to break, glassy foam.	Calm
4	11–16	Moderate breeze	Small waves, becoming longer, fairly frequent white horses.	Slight

The British Canoe Union sea proficiency test assesses an individual's ability to operate in up to force 4 winds. Under their terminology, a proficient paddler is one who can paddle safely as a member of a group within such wind speeds.

Force	Speed (knots)	Description	Sea conditions	Sea state
5	17–21	Fresh breeze	Moderate waves, more pronounced long form, many white horses, possibly some spray.	Moderate
6	22–27	Strong breeze	Large waves begin to form, white crests more extensive everywhere. Probably some spray.	Rather rough
7	28–33	Near gale	Sea heaps up with white foam from breaking waves.	Rather rough
8	34–40	Gale	Moderately high waves of greater length, much foam.	Rough

Force 8 is a sensible upper limit for most paddlers on open water. Remember that it may take 2 days for the sea state to reach its maximum, so conditions in a force 8 can vary a lot.

Force	Speed (knots)	Description	Sea conditions	Sea state
9	41–47	Strong gale	High waves, dense streaks of foam along the direction of wind.	Very rough
10	48–55	Storm		
11	55–65	Severe storm		
12	67+	Hurricane		

be 'veering. If the wind changes direction in an anti-clockwise manner, it is said to be 'backing'. For example a wind would back from south towards the south-east.

The wind blowing across the sea takes time to produce the maximum sea state for that wind speed, although it will only reach this maximum if there is sufficient fetch (see Chapter 12). So although an offshore wind whips up a bit of spray from the water close to shore, it produces only very small wind-blown waves. If you paddle further offshore, the fetch is greater and so is the wave size. Be careful when the wind is blowing offshore as the apparent calm close to shore is deceptive. A capsize victim will be carried into progressively rougher conditions, and any distance paddled from the shore will seem further when it comes to paddling back against the wind. This is called a *weather shore*. With an onshore wind, the prevailing sea state is more apparent from the shore, which is known as a *lee shore*.

Mountains on the coast can greatly affect local winds. Onshore winds are deflected along the shore, and when they approach from within 22.5° of even a low-lying coast, they speed up by as much as 5–10 knots. Offshore winds make detours around mountain blocks. They funnel powerfully through gaps and often sweep along the coast from opposite directions. Wind speeds under these circumstances can increase from a force 3–4 to perhaps a force 9–10 if the mountains are steep. Downdraughts can then be violent and sudden, lifting clouds of spray, and yet the general weather forecast may give little indication of such conditions. So beware of offshore winds near steep, high coasts.

Admiralty pilots frequently note areas that are well-known for violent squalls and areas where katabatic winds are common. Katabatic winds are caused by cold air streaming down from the mountains under gravity, joining forces in the valleys to produce fierce offshore winds where the valleys meet the sea. They are well-known in Greenland, Norway and Antarctica.

Visibility

Visibility is of interest to a sea kayaker. What does the weather forecaster mean when he talks of 'haze', 'mist' or 'fog'? *Haze*, usually caused by dust particles, permits a visibility of at least 2000 m (1¼ miles), although it may be less. *Mist* is water vapour, causing a visibility of less than 2000 m (1¼ miles), although if this drops to below 1000 m (1094 yds) it will be called *fog*.

Otherwise weather reports may describe visibility as excellent (over 30 nautical miles), very good (up to 30 miles), good (up to 10 miles), moderate (up to 5 miles) or poor (less than 2 miles).

Depressions

Depressions are areas of low pressure around which the wind swirls in an anticlockwise direction in the northern hemisphere, and in a clockwise direction in the southern hemisphere. They normally have an associated warm sector containing warm tropical air surrounded by cooler polar air. The leading face of the warm sector is known as the warm front, where moist warm air comes into contact with cooler air and condenses in the form of cloud, and usually rain. The front of the cooler polar air following the warm sector is known as the cold front. This normally swings in from the west behind depressions and carries a shorter period of heavy rain. Cold fronts are often accompanied by a sudden increase in wind speed, and change of wind direction, although the strength of the wind is frequently short-lived.

Anticyclones

Another name for a depression, or area of low pressure, is a cyclone. An anticyclone is an area of high pressure. Winds circulate in a clockwise direction in the northern hemisphere and anticlockwise in the southern hemisphere. Anticyclones frequently become established over land masses and become slow to move, giving longer periods of similar weather. Depressions then tend to track around the anticyclone rather than moving it aside.

Weather forecasts

When you are planning a kayak trip use the long-range and the more accurate short-range weather forecasts issued by telephone, radio, newspapers and television, to build up a good overall picture of what the weather is doing. When you are away from home the telephone pre-recorded forecasts and radio shipping forecasts will give you the best information. The radio has the advantage of portability, and you can listen to a forecast from the comfort of your

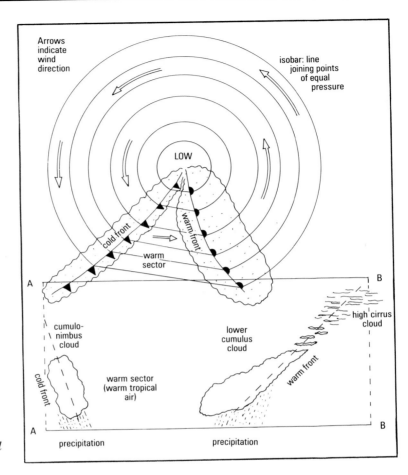

Arrows indicate wind direction

isobar: line joining points of equal pressure

LOW

cold front

warm front

warm sector

A

B

cumulo-nimbus cloud

lower cumulus cloud

high cirrus cloud

cold front

warm sector (warm tropical air)

warm front

A

B

precipitation

precipitation

A northern hemisphere depression with associated warm and cold fronts.

tent on some uninhabited island if you get the time right. The telephone on the other hand may be used at any time . . . if you can find one!

On expeditions further afield, particularly in isolated areas, you may find that there is no weather forecast available, or it might be in a language you cannot understand. In this case you need to be able to read the weather from study of the clouds, changes in wind direction and by reference to changes in temperature and barometric pressure. For this reason I frequently carry a small thermometer and barometer. You do not need to be out in the wilds to practise. Start by comparing the weather forecasts with the weather patterns, picking out the signs of warm fronts and cold fronts, and watching the barometer while depressions pass. You will soon get a feel for the weather.

Air pressure and tides

When the air pressure is high, sea levels are pressed down, and when air pressure is low, sea levels rise. A barometric pressure of 1030 millibars depresses both low and high tide levels by 30 cm (1 ft); a pressure of 980 millibars allows levels to rise by 30 cm (1 ft). Deep depressions moving rapidly over confined areas such as the North Sea, cause not only a rise in the sea level due to the low pressure, but also a movement of water due to the strong winds, which can combine to create *storm surges* of up to 2.4 m (8 ft). Such storm surges, when occurring at spring tides, can cause widespread flooding to lowland areas. In hurricane zones, such as the Gulf of Mexico, hurricane storm surges can raise the sea level above normal by 6 m (20 ft).

Kayak navigation requires common sense to use the elements to assist rather than to hinder you. It requires a combination of pre-planning and final adjustment on the water. For the most part, the kayak is a coastal craft, operating within a few hours' paddling distance of a landing, so you can do much of the planning on shore. You need to consider the three most important influences: the wind, the current and the tidal streams – all of which you can predict fairly well from the forecasts. For longer open passages, for which the normal sea kayak is not the ideal craft, you will need to do your planning day-to-day from your kayak.

Wind

The maximum wind strength that you might consider paddling against will vary depending on your paddling ability, fitness and the distance you wish to paddle. Beginners frequently have difficulty paddling against winds of a strong force 3, whereas fit and experienced sea kayakers have been known to paddle miles against winds in excess of 70 knots when the fetch has been quite short. Such progress is slow and hard work in both examples; better by far to travel downwind if you have the choice, providing you know of a suitable and safe landing place.

Current

Currents are ocean movements that usually flow in one direction constantly, and are not influenced by lunar positions. For example, offshoots of the East Greenland current and the northern extremity of the Gulf stream circle the whole of the Icelandic coast in a clockwise direction, generally at a rate between ½ knot and 2 knots. When the tide is running in the same direction, its speed will add to the speed of the current, whereas when the tide runs against the current its speed will be reduced by the speed of the current. In areas where there is a significant current, it makes sense to make use of it!

Tidal streams

These vary in speed and direction with time, so most journeys can be planned to take advantage of the tides, whichever direction you go.

Paddling speed

Another factor you need to consider when planning journeys on the sea is your paddling speed. This will vary according to your fitness and ability, the type of kayak you are using and the sort of trip you are undertaking. Outside influences such as wind speed and direction, current and tidal streams do not affect your *paddling* speed; they affect your *travelling* speed. It is possible to be *paddling* forwards at 3 knots, yet to be *travelling* backwards as a result of a powerful tidal stream.

Here is a very rough guide to paddling speeds, averaged out over a distance to include brief stops during the day.

General purpose/white-water kayak	2–2.5 knots
General purpose/white-water kayak paddling fast, or sea kayak, paddling leisurely	2.5–3 knots
Sea kayak, paddling fast	3–4 knots
Sea kayak, laden, period of fast paddling without stops	4–5 knots
Sea kayak, lightly laden, sprinting over a short distance	5–6 knots

With experience you will find what paddling pace suits you and the people you paddle with, and will be able to work out your own average speed.

Planning a coastal day trip

When planning a day trip, first decide on the general area in which you want to paddle. This example shows an imaginary section of coast around Homevik. The date for the trip is March 16th. We have decided that we want to paddle about 10 miles or thereabouts. From the road map we have discovered that there is easy access by car to Long Beach, Homevik, Cow Bay, and Deep Cove, (see map) so we could start or finish at any of these points.

From the tide tables find the times of the tides at Homevik. The tables are for Greenport, whereas the tidal information on the chart refers to Homevik. The tidal constant for Homevik from Greenport is add 25 minutes.

High Water Greenport 0605 GMT Add 25 minutes = 0630 GMT HW Homevik.

GREENPORT TIDES

ADD ONE HOUR FROM 01 00 MARCH 26th TO 01 00 OCTOBER 29th

MARCH 2000

| | HIGH WATER | | | | | | LOW WATER | | | | | | SUN | |
| | Morning | | | Afternoon | | | Morning | | | Afternoon | | | Rise | Set |
Date	Time	Ht. mts.	Ht. feet	Time	Ht. mts.	Ht. feet	Time	Ht. mts.	Ht. feet	Time	Ht. mts.	Ht. feet	a.m.	p.m.
1 Wed	03 57	7.3	24.1	16 27	7.1	23.2	10 38	3.2	10.6	23 16	3.5	11.6	07 00	17 49
2 Thu	05 16	7.0	22.9	18 04	6.8	22.3				12 04	3.5	11.3	06 57	17 51
3 Fri	06 56	7.0	23.1	19 45	7.1	23.3	01 04	3.6	11.7	13 47	3.2	10.4	06 55	17 53
4 Sat	08 18	7.6	25.0	20 56	7.8	25.6	02 32	3.0	9.9	15 05	2.5	8.2	06 53	17 55
5 Sun	09 18	8.4	27.4	21 49	8.5	28.0	03 36	2.3	7.6	16 07	1.7	5.6	06 50	17 57
6 Mon	10 07	9.1	29.8	22 34	9.1	30.0	04 31	1.6	5.2	17 01	1.0	3.2	06 48	17 59
7 Tue	10 51	9.7	31.7	23 18	9.6	31.5	05 18	1.0	3.1	17 47	0.4	1.3	06 46	18 01
8 Wed	11 34	10.1	33.1	23 58	9.8	32.3	06 03	0.5	1.6	18 31	0.0	0.1	06 43	18 03
9 Thu				12 17	10.3	33.8	06 43	0.2	0.7	19 12	0.1	0.3	06 41	18 05
10 Fri	00 39	9.9	32.4	12 57	10.2	33.6	07 23	0.2	0.6	19 49	0.1	0.3	06 39	18 06
11 Sat	01 19	9.7	31.7	13 38	9.9	32.6	08 02	0.4	1.4	20 26	0.6	1.9	06 36	18 08
12 Sun	01 59	9.3	30.5	14 20	9.4	30.9	08 42	0.9	2.9	21 04	1.3	4.1	06 34	18 10
13 Mon	02 40	8.8	28.7	15 07	8.7	28.5	09 24	1.5	5.1	21 45	2.1	6.7	06 31	18 12
14 Tue	03 28	8.1	26.6	16 03	7.8	25.8	10 14	2.3	7.4	22 38	2.8	9.3	06 29	18 14
15 Wed	04 33	7.5	24.5	17 23	7.2	23.5	11 29	2.9	9.5				06 27	18 16
16 Thu	06 05	7.1	23.2	19 04	7.0	23.0	00 03	3.4	11.2	13 13	3.0	10.0	06 24	18 18
17 Fri	07 42	7.3	23.9	20 27	7.4	24.3	01 51	3.4	11.1	14 43	2.6	8.7	06 22	18 19
18 Sat	08 51	7.8	25.6	21 22	7.9	26.0	03 10	2.9	9.4	15 46	2.1	6.9	06 19	18 21
19 Sun	09 41	8.3	27.3	22 04	8.4	27.5	04 03	2.3	7.7	16 33	1.7	5.4	06 17	18 23
20 Mon	10 19	8.7	28.5	22 40	8.7	28.5	04 42	1.9	6.3	17 11	1.4	4.5	06 14	18 25
21 Tue	10 52	8.9	29.4	23 11	8.9	29.1	05 16	1.6	5.3	17 42	1.2	4.0	06 12	18 27
22 Wed	11 23	9.1	29.8	23 39	9.0	29.5	05 46	1.4	4.6	18 10	1.1	3.7	06 10	18 29
23 Thu	11 53	9.1	30.0				06 12	1.3	4.2	18 36	1.1	3.6	06 07	18 30
24 Fri	00 07	9.0	29.7	12 21	9.1	29.9	06 39	1.2	4.0	19 02	1.2	3.9	06 05	18 32
25 Sat	00 35	9.0	29.5	12 49	9.0	29.5	07 07	1.3	4.2	19 28	1.4	4.4	06 02	18 34
26 Sun	01 02	8.9	29.1	13 16	8.8	28.8	07 37	1.5	4.8	19 57	1.7	5.4	06 00	18 36
27 Mon	01 30	8.7	28.5	13 44	8.5	27.9	08 06	1.8	5.8	20 25	2.1	6.7	05 57	18 38
28 Tue	02 02	8.4	27.5	14 18	8.1	26.7	08 40	2.2	7.1	20 57	2.5	8.3	05 55	18 40
29 Wed	02 39	8.0	26.3	15 01	7.7	25.2	09 19	2.6	8.5	21 39	3.0	9.9	05 53	18 41
30 Thu	03 31	7.5	24.8	16 03	7.2	23.5	10 14	3.0	9.8	22 47	3.4	11.2	05 50	18 43
31 Fri	04 47	7.2	23.5	17 39	6.9	22.6	11 37	3.2	10.4				05 48	18 45

C 53° 10.0' N 4° 6.2' W

Hours		Dir	Rate (Kn) Sp	Np
Before HW	6	047	0.8	0.4
	5	044	3.2	1.6
	4	046	4.1	2.0
	3	038	4.1	2.0
	2	024	1.9	1.0
	1	225	1.2	0.6
HW		249	3.3	1.7
After HW	1	228	4.5	2.2
	2	225	4.4	2.2
	3	223	4.3	2.1
	4	217	2.6	1.3
	5	211	1.4	0.7
	6	180	0.2	0.1

The format of a tidal information table as it would appear on an Admiralty chart. It relates to position C on the chart.

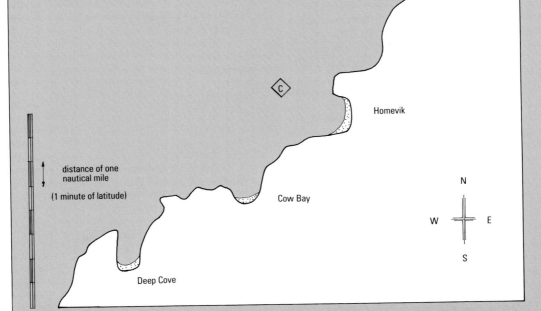

Long Beach

Homevik

Cow Bay

Deep Cove

distance of one nautical mile

(1 minute of latitude)

N
W — E
S

		Neap rate (knots)	Time on March 16th	General direction of tide
HW	HW	1.7	06.30	
Hours after HW	1	2.2	07.30	
	2	2.2	08.30	
	3	2.1	09.30	south-west
	4	1.3	10.30	
	5	0.7	11.30	
	6	0.1	12.30	
Hours before HW	6	0.4	13.30	
	5	1.6	14.30	
	4	2.0	15.30	north-east
	3	2.0	16.30	
	2	1.0	17.30	
	1	0.6	18.30	south-west
	HW	1.7	19.29	

Tidal information for Homevik, gathered from other sources

High Water Greenport 1904 GMT Add 25 minutes = 1929 GMT HW Homevik.

Times are for Greenwich Mean Time. At the top of the page of tide tables note that we do not need to add one hour for British Summer Time before 26th March.

Look at the heights of the tides through March and find out whether March 16th coincides with spring tides, neaps, or falls in between. In this case we have *neaps*.

From the chart (or from tidal stream atlas) find out the direction of the tide through the day. The nearest tidal diamond in this case is ◇ , so refer to the table ◇ for tidal information.

For clarity I have tabulated the relevant information above.

From this information it would seem most appropriate to travel south-west in the morning and to return in a north-easterly direction in the afternoon, gaining the assistance of the tide in both directions.

If we leave Homevik at 0900 and paddle for 3 hours at 2 knots, then we would paddle 6 miles, while the tide carries us a further 2.1 + 1.3 + 0.7 = 4.1 miles. The total distance we would travel is 6 + 4.1 = 10.1 miles. Measuring on the chart (remember to take the scale from the *side* of the chart) we find that 10.1 miles brings us to Deep Cove.

If we leave one hour later, at 1000, and paddle for 3 hours as before, then the tide carries us 1.3 + 0.7 + 0.1 = 2.1 miles. We would cover a total distance of 6 + 2.1 = 8.1 miles, which takes us beyond Cow Bay, but short of Deep Cove.

In this case I decide to leave at the earlier time of 0900, aiming to reach Deep Cove by 1200.

Following a similar procedure for the return journey, note that the tide is strongest during the hours from 1400 to 1700. Paddling carries us 6 miles, and the tide carries us an additional 1.6 + 2.0 +2.0 = 5.6 miles. In 3 hours we would travel 6 + 5.6 = 11.6 miles. We only need to travel 10.1 miles to reach Homevik, so we should arrive back before 1700.

To summarize

Depart Homevik	0900
Arrive Deep Cove	1200
Lunch/exploration	1200-1400
Depart Deep Cove	1400
Arrive Homevik by	1700

Total distance paddled 12 miles
Total distance travelled 20.2 miles

Other considerations that might influence your planning

If there are potential areas of danger, such as tidal races or overfalls within the area, then the journey might have to be planned so as to pass such areas while the tide is weak. Similarly, it might be worth viewing a timetable of ferry times if you are crossing the mouth of a ferry port.

If there is more than one tidal diamond within the section of coast to be paddled, then we have to interpolate to decide how the tide is likely to behave in between.

If the weather forecast indicates a force 4 wind from the south-west, then a journey starting in the afternoon from Deep Cove towards Homevik or even Long Beach would be more sensible. Be prepared to make adjustments to your plans to suit the conditions.

Planning open crossings

There are several ways of planning open crossings, so here are five examples. The different approaches should enable you to make a suitable choice for different situations.

Example 1

First let's consider a crossing to an island in an area where there is either no tide, or which has a long enough slack period to complete the crossing on slack water. First draw a straight line from your starting point to your destination on the chart, A-B. Next measure the distance A-B. In this case the distance is 4 miles. Now find a compass bearing of B from A. You can do this by using parallel rules and transferring from

your drawn line to a compass rose on the chart, reading off the true bearing from the compass rose and correcting it for magnetic variation. Check your course by comparing your compass bearing with the approximate direction you will travel, north, south, east or west, to make certain you have read the compass rose correctly.

When you actually make the crossing, you may paddle on the compass bearing you have worked out, or you may prefer to simply aim at the island, keeping your bearing as a safeguard in case of poor visibility.

In this example, the information in the centre of the compass rose tells us that the magnetic variation in 1997 was 8° 30' west, decreasing by about 10' annually. So for the year 2000 we need to subtract 3 × 10, or 30' from 8° 30', giving us a variation of 8°. As the variation is west of true north we need to *add* the 8° to the true bearing to give us a compass bearing. The bearing we would get if we lined a compass up from point A to point B would be 53°.

The straight line distance from A to B is 4 miles. If you paddle at a speed of 2 knots you will reach the island in 2 hours.

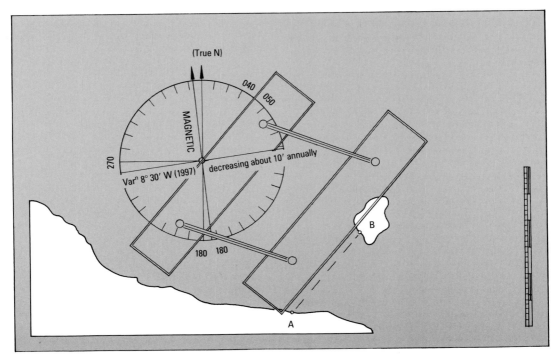

Example 2

A well-used method of making a crossing where the tide runs across your path is to balance out the tide in one direction against the tide in the opposite direction. Your crossing is made over the period straddling slack water. In this example the northerly tide in the hour before high water is compensated for by the tide in the hour of HW.

The compass bearing that you will need will be that of C to D. Your actual path will not be along the line C-D however, as the tide will carry you in this case to the north, and then back to the south. You must follow the compass bearing rather than aiming for the island. Your course will resemble that shown by the dotted line on the diagram, but the distance you actually paddle will be the straight line distance; C-D, of 4 miles. Your paddling time at 2 knots should be 2 hours.

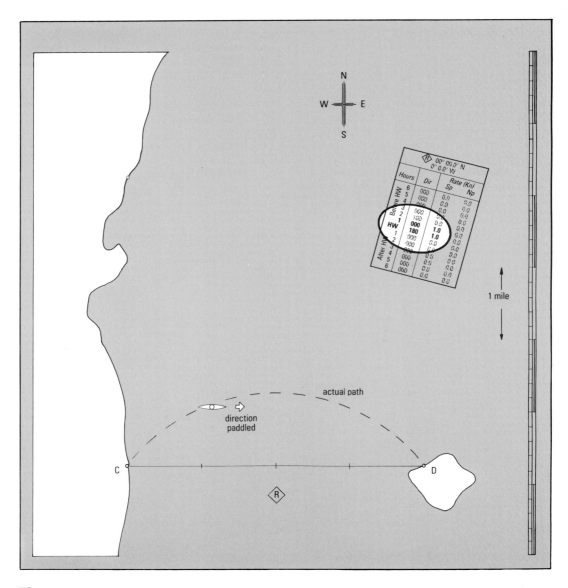

Example 3

A good way of making an open crossing while the tide is running through in one direction only is to depart from a position uptide of your target. Let's take the same island, D, as in the previous example. If the tide is running south at a rate of 2 knots for 2 consecutive hours, then by setting off from a point 4 miles to the north of C, at the point marked E on the diagram, and by paddling on the bearing C-D, you should reach your target of D in two hours. Once again you cannot point your kayak towards the island while you are making the crossing, but you must follow the compass bearing, allowing the tide to sweep you down onto your target.

This method of navigation keeps your paddling distance to a minimum. It can be used to good effect on crossings where the previous method would cause you to arrive at your destination at a time when the tide is running fast. By this method you can arrive at a time when the tide is approaching slack.

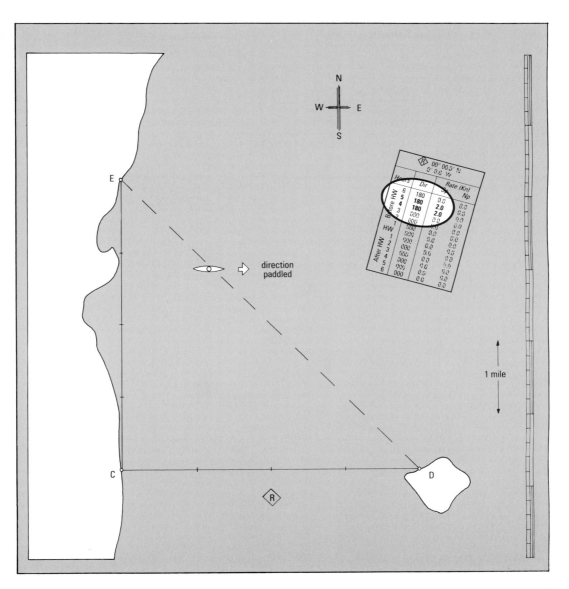

direction paddled

1 mile

Example 4

This method makes a straight crossing by pointing the kayak up into the tide to compensate for the stream. In the first hour of your crossing the tide is travelling at 1 knot at 180°. Measure one mile on the chart from E due south; this is the total effect the tide should have on you in the first hour of paddling. Now measure your paddled distance in that hour, 2 miles, from where your tide has carried you, marked W, to the line E-F, arriving at the point marked G. Repeat the exercise from G for the second paddling hour, to arrive at position H, and in your third hour at position F. Using your parallel rules, transfer from W-G to the compass rose to find the bearing on which to paddle for the first hour. Repeat the process to get bearings for the second and third hours of the crossing.

When you make the crossing, you use three separate bearings, each corrected for magnetic variation, and you change bearings each hour. The actual path you follow is approximately the line E-F, so you could use transit marks to confirm your course.

If you want to use only one compass bearing, measure the distance and direction the tide would take you during the whole crossing, 1 + 1.5 + 1.9 = 4.4 miles, south from the starting point, to the position marked Z on the chart. Take a single bearing from Z to F. Using this single bearing across a tide that is increasing in speed from 1 to 1.9 knots, you can expect to make progress to the north of line E-F to start with, being swept back onto it again by the stronger tide. In this case, you cannot use a single transit to help you navigate, but must follow the compass.

Note that in example 4 you take 3 hours to make a 4-mile crossing, paddling constantly at 2 knots. Your paddled distance is 6 miles. This is not as efficient as in the previous examples, as you are paddling against the tide rather than making use of its power to help you go in the direction you want.

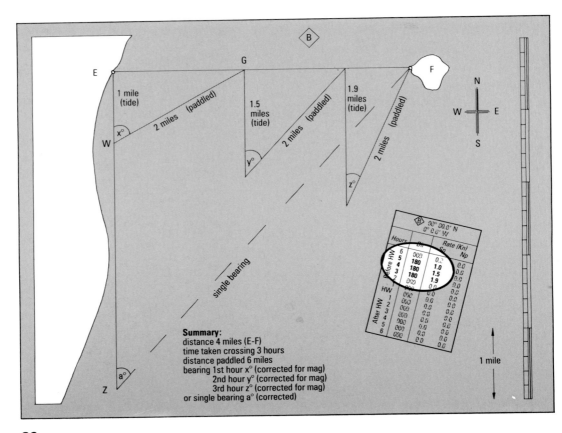

Summary:
distance 4 miles (E-F)
time taken crossing 3 hours
distance paddled 6 miles
bearing 1st hour x° (corrected for mag)
    2nd hour y° (corrected for mag)
    3rd hour z° (corrected for mag)
or single bearing a° (corrected)

Example 5

It is quite usual for the tide to vary in *direction* from hour to hour, so you need to consider both the direction and the speed of the tide. The procedure is the same as in Example 4, but you will need to scan the tabulated tidal stream directions to find the period when the tide will help rather than hinder you. You can still either work from several compass bearings, changing each hour, or adjust to give a single bearing. Note that in the example given, you can make the 4-mile crossing in 2 hours, despite the streams being faster than in example 4, because of their direction.

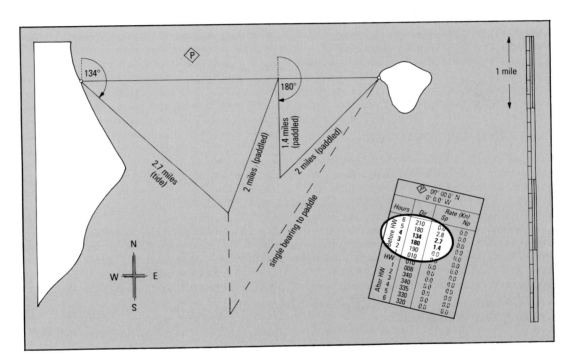

Other navigational techniques

Aiming off

On long open crossings it is often best to aim towards a target uptide of your final destination, so that at the end of the crossing, if you have made a slight error, you only have a downtide run onto your final destination. You may have to paddle a little further but, even in poor visibility, you will know in which direction to turn, even if you are no longer certain about how far you need to go. If you are late, you are still likely to arrive at your target.

If you are making a long crossing that has a strong tidal stream running across your path that you cannot use to your benefit, then it is better to cross during neap tides when any small errors will be minimized.

The use of transits

Transits are the sea kayaker's most useful navigation aid. When making short crossings, keep two objects in line, one behind the other, to maintain a straight course. Adjust the angle of your kayak against the tide or wind to prevent yourself going off line. When you're paddling along a coastline, refer to points in transit alongside to tell whether you are moving forwards slowly or quickly, or indeed whether the wind or tide has effectively stopped you or started to push you backwards. If the nearer transit is falling behind the further one, you are moving forwards; but if the nearer transit is apparently moving forwards in relation to the further one, then you are moving backwards. If there are good transit lines behind you that you can line up with your stern, then use these. Constant reference in all directions will make you much more in tune with and sensitive to changing conditions; this is a mark of a good sea paddler.

Crossing fast tidal streams

When you want to cross a tidal stream the water may be flowing more rapidly than you can paddle. You can ferry glide but you will quickly lose ground. You will need to change your course to approach and cross the eddy line behind your target, and then use the eddy to make up lost ground. Alternatively, paddle across keeping at right angles to the stream all the time, to make the shortest possible crossing. In this case most of the waves will be broadside on to you. Watch for the eddy line, approaching it at right angles.

Using charts and maps afloat

Often Admiralty charts have insufficient information about the land to be able to make good decisions about landing and launching. It can be useful to carry both sea charts and land charts of the area you are to paddle, laminating sections covering the same geographical area back to back between waterproof clear self-adhesive plastic. Some photocopying machines can laminate maps. Alternatively, buy sticky-backed clear plastic sheet, cut out sections slightly larger than your map sections, peel off the backing paper so that the film lies sticky side up on a flat surface, and carefully roll your chart, printed side down, onto the sticky surface. It takes care and practice to get a smooth result that is free from bubbles or 'blisters' between the film and the chart, but it is a process that you can practise at home. Maps need covering on both sides, so it is more economical to place two maps or charts, or one of each, back to back when you laminate.

Before you commit your chart to the waterproof layer, mark on any additional information you feel would be useful in a waterproof ink. If you are cutting your chart into sections of a size that will go beneath your deck elastics, then make certain that each section has got a scale on it so that you can measure distances, and make sure there are reference lines so that you can find north, and thus work out compass bearings. In addition, check through the Admiralty pilot and mark on the times that tidal streams change direction relative to the reference port. Other information, such as your planned time of departure and arrival, and the times at which the tide streams change direction in different places etc. may be marked directly onto your deck with a chinograph pencil or waterproof felt-tipped pen for easy reference. A section of white deck in front of you can be useful for this.

Crossing fast tidal streams

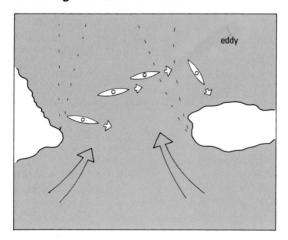

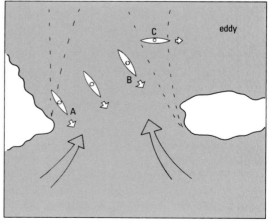

Keeping broadside to the tide stream, and crossing the eddy line at right angles.

Ferry gliding across the stream. Kayak A will make progress sideways, but B is paddling directly into the stream and must change direction in order to cross the eddy line, as in C.

A knowledge of buoyage is important to the sea kayaker, particularly when operating in areas busy with shipping, in estuaries and near harbours. Buoys are used to warn shipping of dangers such as rocks, shoals and overfalls, and to indicate safe channels. They are also used to mark the position of firing range danger areas, sewage outfalls and wrecks. The International Association of Lighthouse Authorities (IALA) have a standard buoyage system for Britain and Europe, known as *System A* and another for the USA, Canada and Japan, known as *System B*. The two systems differ in the colour of lateral (port and starboard) marks.

Lateral marks

These indicate the position of the deepest channel for shipping, usually through island passages and into estuaries and rivers, and make use of port and starboard buoys. Port buoys are can-shaped and are kept to the port, or left, side of a vessel navigating the channel in the direction of buoyage. Starboard buoys are conical and are positioned to mark the starboard side of the channel. Vessels proceeding in the direction of buoyage keep these to their starboard, or right, side.

Where there is a choice of channel, the preferred route is indicated by a buoy with horizontal bands of red and green. The buoy is cone- or can-shaped, indicating the preferred treatment of port or starboard.

Because every set of buoys is used by vessels moving in opposite directions, there has to be a convention in the way they are laid. For rivers, estuaries and other waterways, the direction of the buoyage marking is always the same, from sea to land. In coastal waters, check the arrows on the chart. The symbol used is coloured magenta.

	IALA System A	System B
Port hand buoy		
Shape	Can	Can
Colour	Red	Green
Top mark if fitted	Red, can-shaped	Green, can-shaped
Light if fitted	Red, any rhythm	Green, any rhythm
Starboard buoy		
Shape	Cone	Cone
Colour	Green	Red
Top mark if fitted	Green, cone-shaped	Red, cone-shaped
Light if fitted	Green, any rhythm	Red, any rhythm
Preferred channel to starboard		
Shape	Can	Can
Colour	Red with green horizontal band	Green with horizontal red band
Top mark if fitted	Red, can-shaped	Green, can-shaped
Light if fitted	Red, composite group flashing (2 plus 1)	Green, composite group flashing (2 plus 1)
Preferred channel to port		
Shape	Cone	Cone
Colour	Green with horizontal red band	Red with horizontal green band
Top mark if fitted	Green, conical	Red, conical
Light if fitted	Green, composite group flashing (2 plus 1)	Red, composite group flashing (2 plus 1)

Cardinal marks

These are placed to the north, south, east or west of an area of danger, such as an overfall, bank or shoal. A north cardinal, for example, will be placed to the north of the hazard, and shipping passes to the north of the buoy.

North cardinal mark
Shape: pillar or spar
Colour: black above yellow
Top mark: 2 black cones, one above the other, points uppermost
Light (when fitted): white, VQFl or QFl (very quick flashing or quick flashing)

East cardinal mark
Shape: pillar or spar
Colour: black with a single broad horizontal yellow band
Top mark: 2 black cones, one above the other, base to base
Light (when fitted): white VQFl (3) every 5 seconds, or QFl (3) every 10 seconds

South cardinal mark
Shape: pillar or spar
Colour: yellow above black
Top mark: 2 black cones, one above the other, points downwards
Light (when fitted): white VQFl (6) + long flash every 10 seconds, or QFl (6) + long flash every 15 seconds

West cardinal mark
Shape: pillar or spar
Colour: yellow with single broad horizontal black band
Top mark: 2 black cones, one above the other, point to point
Light (when fitted): white, VQFl (9) every 10 seconds, or QFl (9) every 15 seconds

The position of the points of the cones indicates the position of the black on the buoy. If the top marks are point to point, then there will be black sandwiched between yellow above and below. Both points uppermost indicates black upper-most. The flashing sequences can be remembered by viewing the compass as a clock face. East is 3 o'clock and the flashing sequence features 3 flashes. South is 6 o'clock and the flashing sequence includes 6 flashes. West, at 9 o'clock, features 9 flashes and north features continuous flashing. The choice between quick and very quick flashing is used to distinguish individual buoys that are in close proximity.

Isolated danger marks

An isolated danger mark is used to pinpoint a danger which has navigable water all around it.

Shape: pillar or spar
Colour: black with one or more horizontal broad red bands
Top mark: 2 black spheres, one above the other
Light (when fitted): white, GpFl (2) (Group flashing in sets of 2)

Safe water marks

Safe water marks have navigable water all around and are mid-channel and landfall marks.

Shape: spherical, pillar or spar
Colour: red and white vertical stripes
Top mark (if any): single red sphere
Light (if any): white, isophase (light and dark equal), occulting (dark shorter than light), or one long flash every 10 seconds

Special marks

Special marks are not primarily of navigational significance, although they can fulfil a dual role. They are used to mark special features such as firing ranges and sewage outfalls, and are therefore often of relevance to kayakers.

Shape: optional; can, cone, sphere, spar, etc.
Colour: yellow
Top mark (if any): yellow cross
Light (if fitted): yellow

Buoys in tideways, like moored boats and any other fixed objects, are potentially hazardous. A kayak can get pinned or fold, if the tide is strong. Allow for drift – always aim to pass behind an obstruction rather than in front if you are not sure how strong the stream is.

Never attempt to race across in front of a large vessel. Steam has right of way in narrow chan-nels and, quite apart from the personal danger involved, there is a risk to the ship should the pilot feel he has to try to take avoiding action. His chances of avoiding you in any case are likely to be nil.

Ships turning in marked channels move side-ways considerably as they turn. It is very difficult to anticipate the path of the stern of a turning ship, so it is far safer to wait on the inside of a bend for a ship to pass.

The sea kayak is not ideal for surfing on surf beaches. Better by far are the short wave skis and white-water play boats, which are far more manoeuvrable and present far less danger to other water users. However, a certain amount of surf handling skill is required if you are to launch and land through surf regularly. Many of the techniques, such as paddling out, paddle braces, landing through surf and rolling under waves have been covered elsewhere, but surfing diagonally across a wave has not, and it is a useful technique.

When riding a steep wave straight towards the beach, the nose may bury itself in the water and the wave may throw the kayak end over end. This is known as a 'loop' or 'ender'. Avoid it by surfing the wave diagonally.

The diagonal run

Throw your weight forward and accelerate fast to catch your wave. Next, start to turn your kayak towards one side with a short reverse sweep from the stern. Then, as the kayak starts to turn, quickly put in a stern rudder on your shoreward side while tilting your craft towards the wave. The stern rudder should be angled with the upper edge away from the kayak, stopping it from turning broadside to the wave, and keeping it running downhill. To change direction, reverse sweep from the stern rudder until your kayak is running in the other direction along the wave, then quickly place a stern rudder on the downwave side once more.

Position for a diagonal run

A long, comparatively unmanoeuvrable sea kayak, especially when it's loaded, has consider- able momentum on a wave. Do not practise your surf technique on a beach where you could run down other water users.

Respect the needs of other water users. If you are in doubt about where to land, surfers may be able to give you good advice. Talk to them anyway to foster good relations.

In a sea kayak you can observe wildlife with a minimum of disturbance. Seals, dolphins and whales have all seemingly taken an intelligent interest in observing sea kayakers at close range, and sea birds may often be approached to within a few feet by the sensitive paddler. Your enjoyment will be enhanced if you can identify different species and know something of their habits. Within the scope of this book, I can give only guidelines, using seabirds as an example.

Group seabirds into those of similar appearance, including only those that are commonly found in your area. Bird books will normally give an indication of the range of birds, and a book specifically on sea birds will be easier to work from than a general bird book. Do not worry if similar-looking birds are not grouped together in your book. Your own list is to tell apart birds which look similar.

Now take each group and work out what are the most obvious identifying features. For example, cormorants and shags are 'big dark birds'. Puffins, guillemots and razorbills are 'black and white birds with short plump bodies and short wings that have to be flapped constantly to keep the bird in the air'. All gulls and shearwaters glide easily, gulls soaring well on air currents, yet the fulmar and shearwater have straight-winged flight while the gulls glide on bowed wings.

Finally, within each of your groups, pick out identifying marks that might distinguish each species at a distance. The puffin, for example, has a pale cheek, while the fairly similar guillemot and razorbill do not. The razorbill has a deeper beak profile than the guillemot, so concentrate on this to help you distinguish between the two birds.

Each type of bird has a preferred habitat, and may only be in your area for a limited season. Kittiwakes, for example, nest on the steepest of cliffs, cementing their nests to minute ledges. Out of the nesting season they are seldom found near land. Do not include them in your list of

Below *Observing nature at close quarters.*

suspects for a winter paddle along a sandy shore.

Once you can identify and easily recognize the more common species in your area, you will be more aware of the strangers. By comparing them with birds you know, you can build up a mental picture that will help you identify the stranger when you return home. It may 'fly like a gull' or be 'as buoyant in flight as a tern, but darker in colour', for example. Jotting down observations on your deck with a chinograph pencil will help you remember later.

The identification of species is only the first step, although even this can enhance greatly your enjoyment of sea kayaking. The behaviour, feeding habits and nesting habits are all fascinating to study from a kayak. The more you learn, the more fascinating it becomes. But avoid disturbing birds, especially in their nesting sites where your presence may well lead to the loss of a year's offspring. In winter, waders huddle together and conserve heat. Constant disturbance cools them down. Be sensitive!

If you keep a record of your sightings, with dates, you will know which birds to expect at which season, and where to look for them. You may even find yourself planning special trips away at certain times of year to coincide with the presence of a particular type of bird. I certainly do.

Birds are only one group of creatures that can enhance your enjoyment of paddling. Seals, whales, otters, jellyfish, flora; the avenues are endless. The kayak is a craft that takes you very close to nature. It is up to you to see it.

A young cormorant hitches a ride in the Faeroe Islands.

An expedition can range from the self-contained weekend away to the full-blown trip abroad, operating in inhospitable areas of wilderness. You set your own rules. You can make the kayaking journey the most important part, or simply use your boat as a convenient means to travel in a particular area with some other objective in mind. You can pre-arrange all your food by carrying it all with you, or by depositing food dumps to collect at stages along the journey. You might choose to buy food when and where you can, contributing to the economy of the area through which you pass, or maybe you carry some and hope to catch the rest. Alternatively you may decide to travel light and have a full support team to set up your camp each night, to feed you and to provide you with clean and dry paddling clothing each day. What you must do is to agree on the rules you are going to impose on yourselves so that you do not discover part way through a trip that everyone has different expectations.

Choose an area to paddle. It needs to be within your capabilities. The precise location of your expedition area may be largely dictated by travel or financial considerations. Once you have chosen an area, this may dictate the style of the expedition, the type of craft you use, the distances you need to cover and the time you will need. For example, if the only way you can get to an area is by four-seater plane, you may choose to use inflatable or folding kayaks which will fit inside the plane in preference to 25-ft rigid double sea kayaks. Similarly, if there is a local firm hiring out sea kayaks close to the area you wish to paddle, then you may well find this cheaper than flying out your own kayaks.

Research your chosen area widely. Consult local pilots, charts, maps, and books in the reference library under as many headings as you can think of. Look up information about wildlife, including insects. On one of my early expeditions I failed to do this and we were bitten to pieces by mosquitoes as a result. Find out about the geography, geology, the flora and the people, the history and the political climate, and find out

Below *Sharon Foster with the Lofoten Islands of arctic Norway in the background.*

about previous expeditions to the area. Your research will either whet your appetite or will tell you that it is time to choose a more suitable area. I find the research and planning leading up to an expedition one of the really exciting components. It can extend an expedition by months of anticipation.

Discover discreetly whether there is any established requirement to gain permission from any governing body. Do not ask, if there is not already a precedent set; you will probably only worry a government department into thinking there should be some vetting procedure, and will almost certainly cause many people a lot of time and expense, yourself and those following you included.

In view of your aspirations, chosen type of kayak and the ability of the group, decide upon

Above *A sea kayakers' camp, southern Norway.*

a reasonable daily mileage. Factors such as the likely weather conditions, ocean currents and tidal streams should be considered at this point. It is prudent to allow 'rest days' and 'bad weather' days, when you don't expect to paddle. When we circumnavigated Iceland, we experienced winds of over 30 knots on six consecutive days. Allow yourself a little time in hand, especially if it is not possible to cut your journey short if time runs out. Otherwise ensure that your tickets home allow some flexibility of dates.

Finally, apply a little imagination to the whole project. Often there will be a way of making the expedition more interesting, cheaper, your travel to the area less time-consuming or your time more comfortable. For example, in 1978, Tim Franklin and I cut our kayaks in half to fly to Gander airport in Newfoundland. We saved considerably on the cost of transporting them, made sure that they travelled on the plane with us and, incidentally, set ourselves the interesting task of re-joining them when we arrived. Gander is sited near a large lake, linked by river to the sea, so we simplified and cut the cost of our travel arrangements by paddling our sea kayaks to the sea, before embarking on our sea journey. That extra challenge added considerably to our enjoyment of the expedition; so much so that we both agreed that the expedition had been a success by the time we had reached the sea. Yet the experience was 'incidental' to the main objectives.

Loading for an expedition

Before you leave for an expedition, check that all your equipment will fit in your kayak. Give yourselves extra space by sharing items such as tents, stoves and cooking pans. Discard any inessential food wrappers before you sort your food into 'day packs'. This saves a lot of rummaging through bags at mealtimes and cuts down on the volume of rubbish you have to carry in your craft before reaching a disposal point.

Tents need not be roomy for short trips, but on longer expeditions, where you may be stormbound for days on end, larger tents are much more pleasant. You can spread out in comfort.

Stoves come in a variety of types, using a variety of fuels. Some fuels are not available in some countries. If you run out of alcohol for a spirit stove in the Faeroe Islands, you can only buy it in one place, and then only after you have signed for it. Take more than one type of stove as some excel for quick brews while others are better for long slow cooking.

Stow your equipment in waterproof bags if possible. This adds to the weight, but is much better for loading in wet weather, and in case of a damaged kayak. Compared to many synthetic fibre-filled bags, down sleeping bags are useless if they get wet.

When it comes to actually loading your kayak, carry your empty kayak to the shore, and take your gear down the beach separately in large lightweight bags. Choose your landings with this in mind. Carry your kayak unladen after landing and before launching and you cut out much

of the real risk of injury sustained when carrying heavy and awkward loads on unsteady ground. If you fall when you're carrying a fully laden kayak you can hurt yourself badly and seriously damage your boat. If you must carry a fully laden kayak, make use of as many helpers as possible, preferably at least one at each end and one either side of the cockpit.

Stow heavy items, such as water, fuel and some foods, near the centre of the kayak to improve stability. Similarly, stow lightweight items at the ends. Heavy weights at the ends cause the kayak to plunge and rear. Stow small items in gaps as you load. The loaded kayak should sit in the water on an even keel. If it is heavy at the bow, it will tend to turn up into the wind; heavy at the stern, and it will turn downwind. It should also be loaded so that it does not lie over to one side, otherwise paddling will be quite uncomfortable. Items that you may need during the day, such as your lunch, emergency gear, and a camera, may be stowed in pockets, knee tubes, beside the seat or just inside your hatch. Do not stow items so that they will stop you getting out quickly in an emergency. Stow items that affect your compass – radios, torches, tins and cutlery – as far away from it as possible. If loading seems to be time-consuming and awkward to start with, take heart! It gets easier with practice. When you have been on the move or a few days, items seem to find their own place.

There are many sea paddlers around with a wealth of experience who can advise you on different aspects of planning, and on different parts of the world. In the United States, a good place to to begin research would be Sea Kayaker magazine (P.O. Box 17170, Seattle, WA 98107–0870) or the American Canoe Association (8580 Cinderbed Road, Suite 1900, Newington, VA 22122). In Europe and the United Kingdom, you may want to contact the British Canoe Union Expedition Committee (John Dudderidge House, Adbolton Lane, West Bridgford, Nottingham, NG2 5AS, England); the Advanced Sea Kayak Club (7 Miller Close, Newport, Isle of Wight, England); and the International Long River Canoe Club, which covers sea expeditions as well as long river expeditions (Catalina Cottage, Aultivullin, Strathy Point, Sutherland, Scotland, KW14 7RY). Please include a self-addressed stamped envelope with each inquiry. There are also a number of paddling websites on the Internet.

It was a chilly autumn evening as I loaded my kayak onto my car and drove across Anglesey to Porth Daffarch. By the time I had changed and loaded by kayak it was dark. A group of my friends were paddling somewhere in the area, intending to sleep either in Parliament House Cave or on one of two other beaches, and I had made provisional arrangements to meet them after finishing work, so that I could paddle with them the next day. All I had to do was find them. By the time I launched, a huge orange moon was creeping above the horizon, casting a dim light on the water and gleaming on the crests of the waves. I paddled out from shore, lurching unsteadily over the steep swells as I peered ahead trying to pick out the wave patterns.

On the sea it was eerie. Waves, rebounding from the cliffs, crept up unseen and jolted me as I headed along the cliffs. Each headland and inlet was familiar to me, but in the dark they all seemed to merge together into an indistinct curtain. It was difficult to pinpoint my position as,

tentatively, I made my way along. Was this the narrow bay where my friends said they might possibly stop for the night? I nosed cautiously closer. No! I recognized my position now. I had a little further to go yet.

When I did locate the hidden entrance to the bay I was seeking, I found no sign of my friends. That left two other possible places. Parliament House Cave was the nearer, but I doubted that they would stop there. The tide would be a big one tonight, and the sea was fairly rough, so there would be little or no room to sleep at the back of the cave when the tide reached its highest. To reach the cave I had to pass through Penrhyn Mawr overfalls. They would be heavy tonight. I approached with caution, viewing the dancing phantoms in the pale moonlight and

Below *Fishing from a kayak at night (photo: Drew Delaney).*

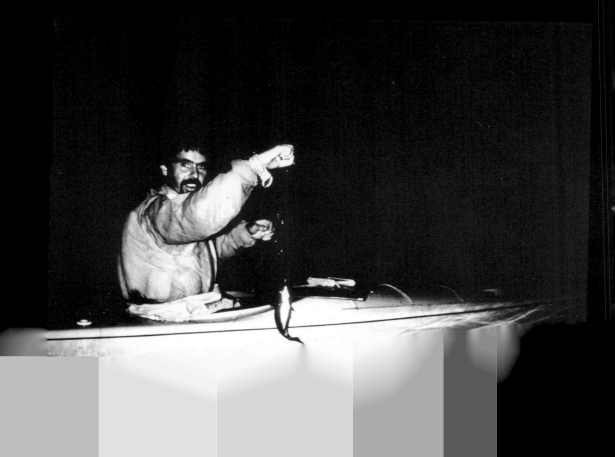

trying to assess their size from a distance. It was impossible. I crept closer, hearing the deep roar of tumbling waves. I began to feel uneasy. It's amazing how much one's paddling judgement relies on sight! It took me a little while to make up my mind. Then I turned around and paddled back.

Paddling in the dark can be truly magical, with brilliant trails of green phosphorescence curving from the bows of your kayak and stirring into vortexes of brilliant stars at every paddle stroke. In moonlight the effect is different. The ghostly light is often sufficient to show you what might be around you, but not enough to show detail.

In inhabited areas, the bright pinpoints of distant lights mingle with closer lights and distances can be hard to judge. If you are approaching one light, and you wish to get an idea of how far away it is, try to line it up with a more distant light. If you now weave a few yards to one side of your course and back again, you will get a better idea of the distance. If the light nearer to you appears to move very little against the background, then it is still some distance away. If however it appears to move much more, then it is closer. Try it out on dry land in daylight. Look at some distant objects and lean your head from side to side. There will be very little apparent movement between the objects. Now look at some objects about 45 m (50 yd) from you and line them up with the horizon and try the same trick. You will begin to see apparent movement. With practice in the dark you will be able to judge relative distances of lights quite well. When you paddle at night you become aware of all sorts of lights, the sky glow above towns, flashing beacons, and lights of cars, boats and houses. You need to be able to identify them if they are to be of service to you.

There is a maritime obligation for every craft at sea at night to carry a bright white light to warn other vessels in order to prevent a collision. Such a light will also be useful for pinpointing your position should you separate from your companions, and to scan possible landing places for dangers. It is also prudent to carry a white hand-held flare which could be used if you need a brighter general light. For example, if a paddler becomes separated from his kayak and paddles in the dark, then a hand-held white flare can illuminate the scene much more effectively, permitting a speedy rescue. Although a white flare is not a distress signal, it is best not to use one unless torches are proving inadequate, as the bright light is easily visible over a distance and may lead to investigation.

Bright lights affect night vision, and there is no legal obligation to display a light constantly in a kayak. A 'glow' is really what we often require rather than a 'light'. Chemical light sticks can provide such a glow. These consist of a glass tube containing one chemical, sheathed inside a plastic tube containing a second chemical. When the outer tube is flexed to break the inner tube, the two chemicals mix, producing a source of light which lasts for many hours (at least for one night). A cheaper alternative, if you are intending to paddle at night more frequently, is a small waterproof torch which you can carry in a pocket to produce the required glow rather than a dazzling light. The batteries can be replaced more cheaply than light sticks.

Keeping together in the dark

One method is for each member of the group to display a prominent light where it can be seen from any direction. Your head is as good a place as any. Check your numbers regularly.

Alternatively, assign a number to each person. From time to time, each person calls out his number in turn. Any missing number can be identified with a person. You may run into problems in the dark from 'extra numbers' caused by passers-by or sea anglers hearing this strange call and joining in.

If the group numbers more than a handful, then you would probably be better off splitting into smaller groups of three or four, with one 'leader' in each group, around whom the others cluster to keep in verbal contact. If each leader displays a 'quiet' light, then he can stay in visual contact with the other leaders, paddling far enough distant to avoid the groups merging.

Caution

Night paddling is disorienting to start with. Begin with practice areas that are utterly familiar to you in the daylight, so that at night you can pick up on all the possible clues available. Choose calm weather, and bear in mind that your progress will be slower in the dark. It is a good idea to pick a time when there is at least a little moonlight before progressing to a really

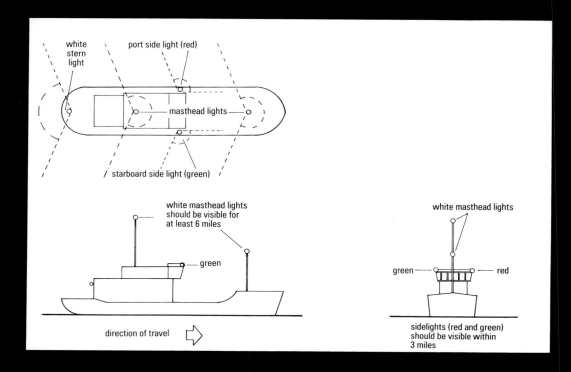

white stern light

port side light (red)

masthead lights

starboard side light (green)

white masthead lights should be visible for at least 6 miles

green

direction of travel

white masthead lights

green — red

sidelights (red and green) should be visible within 3 miles

black night. To practise compass work, try a short triangular or square course, either timing each leg or counting alternate paddle strokes.

White clothing and white on your kayak, and reflective tape all help to make you visible at night. A paddle leash may be a comforting addition to your equipment even if your paddle is marked with tape!

Paddling in rougher conditions is much more serious at night than it is in daylight. Your balance will need to be automatic as you will not see oncoming waves. Approach landings extremely cautiously as when you are beyond the break line your torch beam may not reach as far as the shore. Your calls and shouts don't carry far if it is windy. The glow from your light stick is easily hidden by just a little swell when you are in a trough. By day, in a rough sea, you may be happy to glimpse your paddling partner only occasionally, but such limited contact can be dangerous at night. Consider the consequences of capsizing in the dark under such conditions. Do not overstretch your safety margins.

Finally, night paddling in harbours or areas which have a lot of small boat traffic can be exceedingly hazardous, and should be avoided.

Buoyage at night

The positions of lights on buoys, beacons and lighthouses are shown on charts, together with abbreviations indicating the colour, flashing sequence, height, and the distance at which the lights are visible in good visibility. The navigation lights of shipping are more mobile. It is important to know the basic navigation lights, which must be shown by vessels between sunset and sunrise. Power-driven vessels less than 50 m (164 ft) in length must display a white masthead light, plus two coloured sidelights, red to port and green to starboard. (Port is the left side of the vessel if you are looking ahead from the deck.) Longer vessels must display two masthead lights, with the rear light at a greater height than the forward one. There must also be a stern light visible through the arc in which the masthead lights are not visible.

If you are directly in the path of such a vessel at night you should see two white lights, one directly above the other, with a red light to the right and a green light to the left. To avoid collision, you will need to paddle across the path of the vessel, separating the two masthead lights.

Making use of the wind is a long-established sea kayaking principle. However, the kayak is primarily a paddle-powered craft, so sailing and using kites is an additional facet to the sport rather than an integral part. Sailing with sail or kite is particularly appropriate for open passages and as a means of getting from one interesting paddling area to another with the minimum effort. For this reason I will emphasize the lightweight, simple and unsophisticated rigs rather than the more complex, as the latter readily fall under the auspices of sailing manuals.

Sailing

The simplest sail arrangement is one for downwind use only. All you need is a mast, which fits into a tube set between deck and hull, and a triangular sail, the sail's free corner is attached to a length of line (or sheet, in sailing terms) which you either hold or fasten to a jamming cleat to the side of the kayak. The broader the

kayak, the easier this is to operate. The mast, with sail attached, may be stored in a tube along the back deck when not in use, so that it does not get in the way. A rudder is a useful steering aid, leaving both hands free to handle the sail. If the kayak is to be sailed across the wind, then leeboards or a centreboard will be needed to prevent you from simply being blown sideways. As it is not possible to throw your weight sideways very far in a sea kayak to counter the force on the sail, you have to let out the sail when the wind starts to heel the kayak over.

In a double kayak, your sailing system may easily be more elaborate. A second mast behind the stern paddler (mizzen mast) brings the centre of effort of the sail towards the stern and prevents the kayak from running off downwind all the time, so steering a course across the wind is easier. However, unless you are considering

Below *Sailing kayaks off the coast of Kyushu Island, Japan (photo: Drew Delaney).*

leaving your masts constantly in position, keep your rigging as simple as possible so that you can stow it away quickly with a minimum of difficulty.

Sailing in a catamaran of two kayaks greatly increases the stability. Kayaks can easily be adapted to bolt together and can be powered with single-bladed (canoe) paddles when not under sail. This arrangement is one that I seriously considered for crossing the Hudson Strait in 1981, at the time when there were going to be two of us on the expedition. For the main part of the expedition the single kayaks would have been far preferable but, with a favourable wind, the crossing from Resolution Island to the Button Islands would have been easier under sail. Bolting kayaks together in this fashion had been tried and tested in the Elephant Island expedition in the Antarctic some years prior to this, but in this case the catamarans, made up from double kayaks, were not sailed but paddled, or were powered by outboard motor, and were used primarily to transport large volumes of equipment.

An outrigger is a useful stabilizer for a single kayak. It can be bolted simply to the deck and need not be very heavy or bulky to be effective. Lindemann used an outrigger consisting of half an inner tube of a tyre for his trans-Atlantic crossing in 1956. The kayaks of the nineteenth century were far more suited to sailing than many modern-day sea kayaks. They were clinker-built gaff-rigged craft with a considerable beam, and a large cockpit. Such craft cruised the Scottish islands in surprising numbers and, I imagine, were well suited to the purpose!

Kites

Kites present a totally different challenge from sails. First get your kite! A parafoil shape is probably the best, providing stability, steerability and power. A kite of about $0.93m^2$ ($10 ft^2$) is a good size, fitted with a main line and two steering lines. The steering lines are important as they enable you to steer the kite round, and also to 'trip' it, causing it to stall and fall to the water.

If your kite is the type with an open front section, allow the wind to inflate it to the 'wing' shape, then try to launch it first time without getting it wet. Once wet, it becomes heavy and it is hard to drain all the water out again for a

second attempt. Once well up, the kite finds cleaner winds and is easier to manage. Practise using it on dry land first.

If you decide to run downwind, fasten your kite at a point closer to your bow. If you want to make progress across the wind, bring the attachment point closer to the cockpit and steer the kite well out to the side of your craft. To do this effectively, you need some form of leeboard or centreboard and, nonetheless, may have problems with stability.

If you fasten your kite in its flying position, be aware that the kayak will sail better without you than with you! A sail loses the wind as soon as you fall out of your craft, and generally stops to wait for you, but a kayak pulled by a kite happily carries on without you. Always attach yourself by a safety line just in case. Learn how to stall your kite and carry a knife in case you get out of control and need to drop the kite in a hurry. Once the lines are cut, a kite stalls and falls into the sea where you should be able to retrieve it. Make sure it is adapted to make it float.

Drogues

Drogues can be useful, particularly when attached to rafts of kayaks for checking drift while resting or eating when the wind is not blowing in a useful direction. They can be used in single kayaks but, unless the kayaks are stable, they are awkward items to launch and retrieve and to stow. The best shape is like a flared bucket with a large hole in the bottom, with sufficient buoyancy to keep it lying just below the surface. There should be a line to its widest end, by which the drogue is anchored, and a trip line to the narrower end to help with recovery. It can help to make one line from floating line and the other from heavier line. I met an Irishman who used an old umbrella as a drogue to great effect. If the strain became too great it simply inverted, and when its job was done it folded into the neat 'brolly' that would grace the London commuter. I never saw him in the rain, but I have no doubt that his brolly served a dual purpose on expeditions!

Watch out for the drogue lines catching on your rudder if you have one, or on your deck cargo if your line comes across your deck. Otherwise raise your rudder and attach the drogue line to a loop dropped beneath your hull.